Preface

The research for this report was produced under the auspices of the IFS pensions and retirement saving consortium, to whom the authors are grateful for both financial assistance and useful comments. The members of the IFS pensions and retirement saving consortium are: the Actuarial Profession, the Association of British Insurers, the Bank of England, the Department for Work and Pensions, HM Revenue and Customs, HM Treasury and the Investment Management Association. The authors also thank the Economic and Social Research Council for co-funding through the research grant 'Late Life Work and Retirement' (RES-000-23-0588) and Robert Chote, Richard Disney and Matthew Wakefield for useful comments. Data from the English Longitudinal Study of Ageing (ELSA) and the Labour Force Survey were supplied by the ESRC Data Archive. ELSA was developed by a team of researchers based at the National Centre for Social Research, University College London and the Institute for Fiscal Studies. The data were collected by the National Centre for Social Research. The funding is provided by the National Institute of Aging in the United States, and a consortium of UK government departments coordinated by the Office for National Statistics. Responsibility for interpretation of the data, as well as for any errors, is the authors' alone.

Contents

Executive Summary

This report provides new empirical evidence on the level and distribution of retirement saving in England. For the first time in recent years, we have been able to estimate accrued state and private pension wealth to include in our measures of retirement saving. We use new data on 4,687 individuals aged between 50 and the state pension age taken from the 2002–03 English Longitudinal Study of Ageing. Since there is little existing information on the distribution of accrued pension wealth in Britain, we begin by reporting the level and distribution of pension wealth. We move on to consider total wealth and the relationship between pension wealth and other components of total wealth such as housing and financial assets. We document people's retirement, longevity and inheritance expectations and how these differ across the wealth distribution, before concluding by presenting estimates of the fraction of our sample whose retirement resources appear to fall short of different possible benchmarks for 'adequate' retirement resources. Specific results include the following.

Pension wealth

- Half of those aged between 50 and the state pension age are in families that have pensions (state and private) currently worth £219,300 or more, which would deliver an annual income of around £11,000.
- State pension wealth is far more equally distributed than private pension wealth: the 75th percentile of the distribution of state pension wealth is only 1.8 times larger than the 25th percentile, whereas the 75th percentile of private pension wealth is found to be 16 times greater than the 25th percentile.
- But, on average, private pension wealth is almost twice the size of state pension wealth.
- Overall, therefore, there is substantial inequality in pension wealth – the 10 per cent of individuals with the most pension wealth have, on average, £874,000, whereas the 10 per cent of individuals with the least have, on average, just £48,000.
- Those not in work fall into two groups. Individuals not in paid work who classify themselves as retired have substantially higher pension wealth than those still in the labour market. The remaining individuals not in paid work have substantially lower pensions than their counterparts in the labour market.
- Multivariate analysis shows that the characteristics associated with higher levels of pension wealth are being a member of a couple, having no long-standing health problem, having higher levels of education and having higher levels of non-pension income.

Total wealth

- Half of the individuals in our sample have total wealth of under £400,000. One-in-ten individuals have wealth worth more than £1,000,000 and one-in-ten have wealth worth less than £110,000.
- On average, pension wealth and non-pension wealth do not act as substitutes for each other – those with higher levels of non-pension wealth also tend to have higher levels of pension wealth.
- The composition of total wealth varies considerably across the wealth distribution. Mean total family wealth for the poorest 10 per cent of individuals is just £66,000, about £57,000 (87 per cent) of which is state pension wealth. In contrast, among the richest tenth of the population, only 7 per cent of total wealth is in the form of state pension wealth, with 37 per cent being held in private pensions, 21 per cent in owner-occupied housing and 34 per cent in other private wealth.
- As with pension wealth, we find that those not in paid work who classify themselves as being retired have the highest level of wealth, followed by those still in paid work, with those not in paid work who do not report being retired having the lowest level of total wealth, on average.

Expectations of future circumstances and resources

- Individuals with low current levels of wealth, on average, are also less likely to expect future events to occur that might boost their future resources:
  - The wealthiest 10 per cent of individuals anticipate on average that there is a 31 per cent chance they will receive an inheritance of at least £10,000, whereas the poorest 10 per cent of people report on average only a 13 per cent chance of receiving such an inheritance.
  - Men aged 50–59 in the bottom wealth decile report on average only a 37.3 per cent chance of working at age 60, compared with the average across all wealth deciles of 55.3 per cent.
- Unless they expect to increase their pension contribution rate between now and when they retire, individuals appear, on average, over-optimistic about the income that they will receive from their private pensions when they retire. The average income that individuals are predicted to receive from private pensions that they are yet to draw is around £8,600 per year. However, on average, individuals are expecting income of around £10,500 from these pensions – an apparent average overestimate of around 20 per cent.
- Nearly half of all individuals who have a private pension from which they are yet to receive income overestimate the amount that they will receive from those pensions by at least 30 per cent. This group represents around a fifth of all individuals aged between 50 and the state pension age.
- Controlling for other characteristics, individuals who overestimate their future pension income are *more* likely to report a higher chance of having inadequate resources at some point in the future.

Who is at risk of 'inadequate' resources in retirement?

- Even if all individuals aged between 50 and the state pension age retired immediately, we predict that once they reach the state pension age, the majority (57.2 per cent) would have net income from their pensions alone of at least 67 per cent of their current net income.

- Taking into account individuals' own expectations of the timing of their retirement and their receipt of inheritances in the future, we estimate that before claiming any entitlement to the pension credit, 7.7 per cent of those aged between 50 and the state pension age would have retirement resources worth less than the level of the pension credit guarantee.

- If we include entitlement to the pension credit, we estimate that 11.3 per cent (or just under 850,000 individuals in England) would have net resources when they reach the state pension age worth less than 67 per cent of their current net income. A further 11.8 per cent would have net resources of between 67 and 80 per cent of their current net income.

- Individuals who have high current income (for example, those in paid work) are more likely to be at risk of having low replacement rates in retirement. In contrast, it is the lifetime poor (for example, those with low levels of education, those in poor health and those out of work who do not consider themselves retired) who are most at risk of having retirement incomes below the pension credit guarantee, even if their retirement income is predicted to be high relative to their current income.

CHAPTER 1
Introduction

Retirement saving through pensions in the UK has become a major policy issue. Unlike in many other European countries, however, the concern in the UK is not the sustainability of state pension funding in the presence of impending population ageing. Rather, the concern is the adequacy of private saving to maintain a reasonable standard of living in retirement, as the state system is projected to become progressively less generous relative to both average incomes and what it would have been in the absence of reforms made in the 1980s and 1990s.

Raw projections of the cost of the state pension system appear affordable as a result of previous pension reforms that have cut pension benefits for future pensioners. The changes to the State Earnings-Related Pension Scheme as a result of legislation passed in 1986 and 1995, coupled with the formal indexation of state pension payments to growth in prices rather than to the greater of growth in prices or earnings (since the early 1980s), and the planned increase in the female state pension age, have substantially reduced the projected future cost of the system.[1] But as a result of these reforms, the amount that many individuals can expect to receive from the state when they reach retirement will now be lower, especially since any additional state spending that there has been has been targeted on those with the lowest incomes through more generous means-testing. By 2054, state transfer payments per pensioner as a proportion of national income are projected to be just two-thirds of the level they were in 2004.[2] Private retirement saving is therefore taking on an increasingly important role in ensuring adequate consumption in retirement. Consequently, the nature of the policy debate in the UK is somewhat different from that elsewhere in Europe, focusing on the appropriate balance between targeting (reduced) state pension spending on those who need it most and facilitating greater private pension saving by the rest of the population.

The key policy issues surrounding pensions in the UK therefore relate to the adequacy of future pensioner incomes which, in turn, has led to a focus on increasing the labour market participation of older working-age individuals and getting individuals to save greater amounts than earlier cohorts (either voluntarily or through attempts to compel individuals to increase their retirement saving). These issues are predicated on the assumption that a large number of individuals in the UK are not currently saving 'enough' to fund their retirement. Whilst this seems plausible for some individuals, a lack of suitable data has meant that there is, as we discuss below, relatively little (if any) convincing empirical evidence to back up this assumption to date. This report provides some detailed new evidence pertaining to this question, and considers the adequacy of financial resources for retirement at the microeconomic, or individual, level. We also discuss some of the issues surrounding people's plans for future labour market participation.

---

[1] For a discussion of the reforms to state pensions since 1975 and their implications, see, for example, Attanasio et al. (2004) or Disney and Emmerson (2005).
[2] Source: Emmerson, Tetlow and Wakefield, 2005.

Assessing the adequacy of retirement saving is a complex issue and it is important to remember that an 'adequate' level of retirement saving may be very different from the level that would be implied by economically 'optimal' consumption and saving behaviour. Economic models of consumption and saving behaviour have the property that the 'optimal' level (and type) of saving for an individual will depend on a host of individual-specific factors. These include past outcomes, detailed current circumstances and all relevant expectations of the future, including expected financial, demographic and health circumstances, as well as any uncertainty surrounding these expectations. As such, it is impossible to say from macroeconomic data whether people are saving 'optimally' for their retirement, and even using individual-level data it is extremely hard to assess the optimality of individuals' saving choices in a rigorous manner.

There are also many different ways to transfer resources over the life cycle, which, after all, is the reason households save and borrow. Durable goods, intergenerational transfers (either between generations whilst alive or through bequests and inheritances) and government transfers all reduce the need to save for one's retirement, as would simple (anticipated) changes in preferences as people age. To make factors more complicated still, life is inherently uncertain and therefore individuals may be making *ex-ante* adequate provision for their retirement but, due to unforeseen outcomes, may still not end up with 'enough' to fund their retirement in a manner comparable to their working lives. Depending on individuals' impatience and their preferences for smoothing their resources over the life cycle, economically optimal saving behaviour may end up, *ex post*, yielding low retirement resources at times when asset market or labour market returns are particularly low. There could still be a rationale for government intervention, however, either on the grounds of distributional considerations or in order to correct a specific market failure – for example, incomplete insurance markets which could have prevented individuals from insuring against future risks at a fair price.

Scholz, Seshadri and Khitatrakun (2004) provide the most complete investigation of these issues to date but their analysis pertains to the US. To summarise, they solve a complicated optimal life-cycle consumption saving model separately for every individual in a large random sample of US households and compare the assets that the individuals actually have with the levels that they would be predicted to have were they saving 'optimally'. In short, despite the commonly held view that the US baby boomers need to save more, there is relatively little (*ex-post*) evidence of under-saving – only 18.6 per cent of the households have savings (including pensions and housing) that are lower than optimal, and amongst these the shortfall is relatively small (around $5,700 on average).

Whilst related, our goal in this report is not so ambitious, since even the basic empirical evidence base in the UK is considerably weaker than that in the US. Despite the (in)adequacy of retirement saving being a policy issue of increasing importance in recent years, almost nothing is actually known about the aggregate or disaggregate wealth holdings of different groups in the population. The hindrance to the pension adequacy debate posed by data limitations was, for example, identified by the Pensions Commission (2004, appendix A) as one of the major obstacles to developing a comprehensive picture of the under-saving problem in the UK. This gap in the evidence base was also identified in the government's recent Green Paper on savings (Department for Work and Pensions, 2002) and may be on the way to being closed with the ongoing development of a new Wealth and Assets Survey.[3]

This report assesses for the first time the distribution of both pension and non-pension wealth amongst the population aged between 50 and the state pension age (SPA) in England. We focus on this age group for a number of reasons. First, high-quality microdata on both pension and other wealth do not yet exist with which to carry out this exercise for younger individuals. Second, focusing on older, but still pre-SPA, individuals is also likely to be most relevant for medium-term policy discussions. Younger individuals have a long time horizon over which their behaviour (and indeed policy) could change. But the current wealth and pension arrangements of older individuals are likely to be a good indicator of the resources they will have available to them throughout their retirement (and their retirement expectations are also likely to be better formed than those of the younger groups). The group we focus on here will be reaching the SPA within the next 15 years, and therefore any policy reform aimed at influencing their retirement or saving behaviour would need to be implemented relatively quickly. In our conclusions, we discuss briefly what lessons can be learned from this age group for the longer-term policy issues surrounding the retirement saving of those cohorts currently under the age of 50.

In Chapter 2 of this report, we describe the key features of the data we use for our analysis. These data – the ongoing English Longitudinal Study of Ageing – allow up-to-date and detailed individual- and household-level analysis of pensions and retirement saving in England for the first time. Since the level and distribution of pension wealth amongst the cohort currently approaching retirement in England have not previously been studied, Chapter 3 begins our empirical analysis by describing in some detail the distribution of current state and private pension wealth across all individuals, and across subgroups of the population. We show the extent to which certain characteristics are associated with particularly high or low levels of pension wealth.

Individuals can use assets from a number of sources to fund their desired level of consumption during retirement, so looking solely at pension wealth will fail to reflect accurately the true level of resources available to individuals for their retirement. First, individuals may have liquid financial assets that they can use for consumption. Second, individuals (particularly the self-employed) may have other wealth or physical assets that they can sell at retirement. Third, individuals could release some or all of the value of their owner-occupied housing wealth to fund retirement consumption, though there is some debate as to how willing individuals will be to do this. So, for some people at least, pension saving will not be the only source of funds for retirement. For this reason, Chapter 4 looks at the distribution of wealth between these various broad asset types and finds that the relative importance of different assets (particularly state pension wealth) varies by total wealth level. Pension wealth represents the largest component of retirement resources, of course, but we also show that there is no evidence that those with low

---

[3] Specifically, one of the Office for National Statistics's 2004 Spending Review Performance Management Framework Targets, aimed at improving the quality of statistics in this area, is that '(subject to establishing viable partnership funding arrangements) we will develop and complete the fieldwork required for a comprehensive Wealth and Assets Survey, with results to be published in 2007' (http://www.statistics.gov.uk/about_ns/ONS/2004_spending_review_sda.asp).

pensions have offsetting high levels of other assets. Indeed, the correlation across holdings of asset types is strongly positive.

The evidence here provides a detailed analysis of the possible extent of under-provision of resources amongst the cohort of people approaching retirement. In doing this, we attempt to control, albeit very crudely, for individuals' needs for retirement saving as well as the stock of assets they have available to them. However, rather than model optimal retirement saving needs (like Scholz, Seshadri and Khitatrakun (2004)), we simply use individuals' self-reported expectations of the future to provide a benchmark. Hence, in Chapter 5, we examine individuals' expectations to see whether low-wealth individuals have high expectations of future events (such as receiving an inheritance, working longer or dying younger) that would reduce the resources they currently need to hold in order to fund any given level of future retirement consumption. We find that this largely is not the case, particularly as regards expectations of receiving an inheritance and working longer. In this analysis, we also look at the amount of private pension income individuals expect to receive and compare this with the level of income they are likely to receive. These results suggest that individuals are, on average, overestimating the pension income that their private pensions are likely to provide, so we briefly examine the factors that are associated with apparently over-optimistic expectations of private pension income. Finally, we look at the extent to which current wealth levels are associated with more general self-reported worries about the adequacy of retirement incomes.

Chapter 6 attempts to bring together the analysis of previous chapters and provides a breakdown of the population aged between 50 and the state pension age according to the 'adequacy' of their retirement saving. In order to do this (and since we are identifying 'adequate' as opposed to 'optimal' retirement saving), we need to specify a definition for adequate retirement resources. For each member of our sample, we calculate their projected retirement income and compare it with a number of benchmarks currently discussed in the policy debate: either a flat-rate 'minimum' income level equal to the level of the pension credit guarantee or a variety of projected replacement rates (the income received in retirement as a fraction of the income received while working). We then assess what fraction of the population will be 'at risk' of falling below the measure of adequate retirement income according to each definition.

It is worth restating that we are in no sense evaluating whether individuals' savings are optimal (as in the Scholz et al. (2004) paper, for example) given their circumstances and preferences. In addition, since replacement rates are typically expressed as a fraction of current incomes, there are conceptual differences between definitions of adequacy based on replacement rates (i.e. looking at relative income drops) and those based on the absolute level of retirement resources. Once one has specified the degree to which the goal of government pension and retirement saving policy should be poverty alleviation as opposed to income replacement, the value of each type of benchmark becomes clearer. As this debate is ongoing (and is likely to be so for some time), we present both types of benchmark in our distributional analysis. Since, within each broad type of benchmark, the choice of the adequacy level is still somewhat arbitrary, we also present a complete description of the distribution of predicted replacement rates and predicted retirement incomes so that other potential adequacy levels can be assessed.

In addition, our analysis considers how different assumptions relating to retirement ages, the use of housing wealth and the possible receipt of inheritances might change estimates of the fraction of the population 'at risk' under the various adequacy definitions. We find that those whom we identify as 'at risk' are statistically significantly more likely to expect inadequate resources at some point in the future than those with higher projected retirement resources. Finally, we discuss the socioeconomic dimensions in which the 'at-risk' group looks different from the population at large. Chapter 7 summarises our findings and concludes with some thoughts for policy debate, both in terms of implications for cohorts soon to approach retirement and in terms of more speculative conjectures that relate to the longer-term policy debate about the adequacy of retirement saving for cohorts that are currently at younger working ages.

CHAPTER 2
The English Longitudinal Study of Ageing

Until very recently, it was not possible to carry out the analysis we provide in this report due to a lack of appropriate survey data in the UK. Existing surveys were either out of date (i.e. the British Retirement Survey, in which respondents were first interviewed in 1988–89 and followed up in 1994) or else contained only limited data on wealth and, in particular, pension wealth (i.e. the Financial Resources Survey and the British Household Panel Survey). Thankfully for research on savings, pensions and wealth accumulation, this situation has begun to change.

The analysis we present here is based entirely on a new data source – the English Longitudinal Study of Ageing (ELSA).[1] ELSA is an ongoing project that is collecting repeated observations of the health, income, wealth and social and family circumstances of a representative sample of around 12,000 individuals aged 50 and over in households in England. The first 'wave' of ELSA data was collected between March 2002 and March 2003, and it is these data that are used in this report. Subsequent waves will provide the possibility of identifying changes over time, following wealth and health trajectories as people retire, and even making comparisons across cohorts since new cohorts of sample members will be introduced as the existing sample ages. A full description of the first wave of ELSA data and a summary discussion of its motivation and design can be found in Marmot et al. (2003).

For our purposes, one of the particular strengths of the ELSA data is the number of detailed questions on both current and past pension arrangements along with all other forms of financial assets, wealth and debts. Whilst collecting data on such items is traditionally thought to be problematic, recent advances in survey and statistical methodology have now made such measurements more feasible and worthwhile. In particular, the ELSA questionnaire follows innovations in other studies outside of the UK by employing 'unfolding brackets' to reduce substantially the problem of non-response for such financial variables.[2]

Since we are to analyse the wealth and pension data in some detail, it is worth describing briefly how our financial measures are computed. Taking non-pension wealth first, ELSA contains detailed questions on individual components of financial, physical and housing wealth for each 'financial unit' in the sample. The financial unit is defined as the individual for single people or as the individuals for couples who keep their finances separate from their partner, and as the couple otherwise. For observations with missing or banded (bracketed) data for an item of wealth, we predict a precise value for that wealth category using conditional hot-deck imputation, i.e. by choosing at random a value from those values reported by the sample of similar financial units (where 'similar' is defined by characteristics

---

[1] Marmot et al., 2005.

[2] With this methodology, individuals who report 'don't know or refuse' to a financial question are asked a succession of questions loosely of the form 'Is it more or less than £x?' so that researchers can identify a range of assets in which the individual's assets lie. This range can be used directly in statistical modelling, or else as a basis for subsequent imputation of the original missing data.

such as age, gender, education, employment status and wealth level – the last only in cases for which we know the range in which wealth lies). The values obtained are then summed across families (where a family is defined as being a couple or a single individual) and attributed to all individuals within that family.

The calculations of pension wealth are somewhat more complicated since respondents are not asked direct questions about their pension wealth in the ELSA questionnaire. In addition, since a pension is a flow of income that will be paid until the individual dies, this flow of (future) income needs to be turned into a 'stock' of wealth if we are to compare it with other types of wealth or to include it in an aggregate wealth measure.

There are two main sources of pension wealth – wealth from state pensions and wealth from private pensions. The wealth figures for both these types of pensions are essentially calculated by summing the stream of income that the individual will receive between their retirement (or the state pension age (SPA) in the case of state pensions or now in the case of private pensions already in payment) and their death, having used discounting to take account of the fact that the income will not be received until some time in the future. The pension wealth figures assume a real discount rate of 2½ per cent and assume that all individuals die at their age- and gender-specific life expectancy, obtained from actuarial life tables. Of course, many further assumptions need to be made. A brief description follows, but for greater detail on the calculation of these pension wealth figures and the sensitivity of the estimates to the assumptions made, see Banks, Emmerson and Tetlow (2005).

State pension wealth comprises wealth from the basic state pension (BSP) and wealth from the state second-tier pension (SERPS or S2P). In order to calculate BSP wealth, assumptions had to be made about the individual's previous labour force participation at all ages between 16 and their current age. To calculate SERPS/S2P wealth, assumptions had to be made not only about labour force participation but also about earnings in all years between 1978 and the present. Since ELSA wave 1 does not contain any retrospective information on employment and earnings, we follow previous studies (for example, Blundell, Meghir and Smith (2002)) and assume that (a) individuals were in employment between leaving full-time education and leaving their last job and (b) individuals earn the same wage relative to the median for their gender (controlling also for their cohort and their education group) over their life cycle. Under these assumptions, we can calculate past earnings for each member of the ELSA sample using cohort- and education-specific earnings profiles estimated from the Family Expenditure Survey over the period 1978 to 2002. Using these employment and earnings histories, it is then possible to calculate state pension wealth for each household in 2002 by applying the rules of the various elements of the (past and present) BSP and SERPS/S2P regimes to the earnings history of each sample member.

Private pension wealth can take the form of either employer defined benefit (DB) or defined contribution (DC) plans or individual DC pensions (including personal pensions and stakeholder pensions). The ELSA questionnaire includes questions relating to up to two current pension plans and up to three past plans of which an individual is no longer a member. Using information on the length of membership, the plan rules and a forecast for the individual's final salary, it is possible to calculate the income from a DB pension that the individual would receive during retirement and hence their discounted pension wealth in 2002. In the case of DC plans, the accrued pension fund value is collected directly from the respondent and uprated to take account of assumed potential growth in the value of the fund, and assumed additional contributions, between the current date and retirement. This income stream is then converted into a value for discounted pension wealth.

The final key variable in the pension wealth equation is the date of retirement. Since the sample of individuals used in this analysis are aged between 50 and the SPA, there may well be substantial differences in pension wealth according to when, in this period, the individual actually retires. Since this is both an important margin for analysis and a choice for the individual concerned, we calculate pension wealth on four bases for the analysis that follows.

In Chapters 3 and 4, where we are looking at the analysis of current wealth, we use a measure of currently accrued pension wealth – in other words, we look at what wealth an individual would have if they retired immediately after the ELSA interview, i.e. in 2002–03. This is, in general, a lower-bound estimate of what an individual's pension wealth will be at retirement, but an accurate reflection of the importance of pension wealth in their current portfolio.

In Chapters 5 and 6, where we are considering the implications of current wealth for retirement living standards, we also consider pension wealth computed on the basis that all individuals are in paid work (and continue to contribute to their pension at the same rate) right up until the SPA. As this may also be unrealistic (since we know that those in the sample age group who are currently out of work are unlikely to return to work), we compute an intermediate measure where those individuals currently in work are assumed to stay in work until the SPA and those currently out of work are assumed to remain out of work. Even this may overestimate the proportion remaining in work until the SPA, since many of those in work are likely to leave the labour market before then. So we also calculate a probabilistic measure that takes into account individuals' own expectations of working in the future.

Having calculated each individual wealth component, we then aggregate the financial data up to the family level for the purposes of analysis. Hence our measure of wealth can be thought of as family wealth. That is to say, although our tabulations are on an individual basis (i.e. by individual's age, gender, education etc.), the wealth that the individual is considered to have access to will be the total wealth of the couple if they are married or living as married. We can then create the broad categories of wealth used for the analysis within this report. Table 2.1 summarises these categories. For the majority of our analysis, we will be working with one of the four definitions of wealth in the lower panel of the table. In order to see what is included in each definition, the table also shows how each category breaks down into its constituent parts.

Two final elements of the ELSA data are worth discussing briefly before we move on to our analysis. These are the measures of retirement expectations and the measure of numerical ability that we use in the analysis presented in Chapters 5 and 6. ELSA is unique in Britain in containing quantitative information on individuals' expectations and ability in conjunction with the data relating to their financial circumstances. Once again, the measures are relatively novel and warrant some description.

Table 2.1
Wealth definitions used throughout this report

Category	Included assets
State pension wealth	Basic state pension State Earnings-Related Pension / State Second Pension
Private pension wealth	Employer pension Personal pensions and other defined contribution pensions (e.g. S226 plans and stakeholder pensions)
Net financial wealth	Interest-bearing accounts at banks and building societies National Savings and premium bonds Individual Savings Accounts and Personal Equity Plans Stocks and shares Government, corporate and local authority bonds Investment trusts and unit trusts *less* Outstanding loans or debts
Net housing wealth	House value (principal residence) *less* Outstanding mortgage debt
Business and property wealth	Non-owner-occupied housing wealth Property and land Antiques and collectables Covenants and trusts Business wealth

Broad definition	Included categories
Pension wealth	State pension wealth + Private pension wealth
Other wealth	Net financial wealth + Business and property wealth
Non-housing wealth	*Pension wealth* + *Other wealth*
Total wealth	*Non-housing wealth* + Net housing wealth

Individual expectations of future events are collected on a 'per cent chance' basis – respondents are asked to evaluate the likelihood of various events on a scale of 0 to 100 where '0 means there is absolutely no chance the event will happen, and 100 means you are certain the event will occur'. Information is collected in this manner for, amongst other things, the self-reported chances of living to older ages, of receiving inheritances or leaving bequests of varying amounts, of working at later ages and of financial resources not being 'enough to meet future needs'.

In order to measure numerical ability, we construct a simple four-category variable representing the respondent's ability to answer the five basic questions (which involve successively more complex 'everyday' numerical calculations) that are delivered in the ELSA interview. As a guide to the levels being indicated, the most numerate group successfully answer a compound interest question, and the next most numerate group successfully answer a question requiring percentages. Between them, these highest two numeracy groups make up a relatively large fraction of the population, having a combined prevalence of 37.3 per cent in the whole population aged 50 and over and of 46.5 per cent in the group aged 50–64. Less than half of these individuals, however, correctly answer the compound interest question, and hence the prevalence of the highest numeracy group alone is substantially lower.

Finally, all the financial data used in this report have now been deposited in the UK Data Archive as ELSA derived data-sets which supplement the core interview files. As such, all the analysis presented in what follows, or any variants on that analysis, can be carried out from the public-use ELSA data without having to reproduce the somewhat arcane calculations and imputations for financial and pension wealth described above. Further details, along with the data themselves and details of how to access them, are available at

http://www.data-archive.ac.uk/findingData/snDescription.asp?sn=5050.

CHAPTER 3
The Nature of Pension Arrangements and the Distribution of Pension Wealth

Previous work has shown that financial wealth is very unevenly distributed across households in Britain. Disney, Johnson and Stears (1998), Banks and Tanner (1999) and Banks, Smith and Wakefield (2002) all show that this was the case across all age groups in Britain. Banks, Karlsen and Oldfield (2003) found the same result across families aged between 50 and the state pension age (SPA) in England using the ELSA data.

To date, the only study that has allowed examination of the distribution of pension wealth across families is the British Retirement Survey, which interviewed a sample of individuals aged between 55 and 69 in 1988–89 (some of whom were re-interviewed in 1994). Using data from this study, Disney, Johnson and Stears (1998) show that pension wealth was a large component of overall wealth. They calculate that mean total wealth in 1988–89 was £212,400, with 25 per cent of mean wealth held in occupational pensions, 32 per cent in state pensions, 35 per cent in housing wealth and just 8 per cent in financial wealth.[1]

Lack of sufficient information has meant that it has not been possible to produce more up-to-date statistics on the distribution of pension wealth and therefore total wealth. The circumstances of those now approaching retirement might be quite different from those of earlier cohorts, not least due to policy changes (such as the introduction of personal pensions, PEPs, TESSAs and ISAs, and substantial reforms to state pensions) and large fluctuations in asset prices (in particular, house prices, equity prices and annuity rates) over the intervening period. Therefore this chapter presents new evidence on the distribution of pension wealth amongst those now approaching the SPA. Section 3.1 provides statistics on the distribution of pension wealth, which is then decomposed by type of pension wealth in Section 3.2. Section 3.3 looks at the association between pension wealth and other individual characteristics, while Section 3.4 provides estimates of pension income from pension wealth accrued to date as a share of current employment income for those currently in paid work. We then turn in Chapter 4 to show how pension wealth is correlated with non-pension wealth, and to provide details on the distribution of total wealth.

3.1 Distribution of pension wealth

Individuals can have pension wealth from both private pensions and state pensions. Table 3.1 shows the distribution of state, private and total pension wealth for all individuals aged between 50 and the SPA in ELSA. The pension wealth figures

---

[1] Source: Authors' calculations based on table 5 of Disney, Johnson and Stears (1998).

Table 3.1
Distribution of family pension wealth (£000s)

	Mean	p10	p25	Median	p75	p90
State pension wealth	102.9	50.5	71.6	98.6	129.4	164.5
Private pension wealth	189.2	0	16.9	109.4	271.1	473.7
Total pension wealth	292.2	73.1	120.3	219.3	380.0	583.3

Notes: Sample size = 4,687. One observation per individual aged between 50 and the SPA. Further details of the calculation of both state and private pension wealth using ELSA data can be found in Banks, Emmerson and Tetlow (2005).

(throughout this report) refer to the total pension wealth of the family. Table 3.1 shows that the distribution of private pension wealth is far more skewed than the distribution of state pension wealth. Mean state pension wealth (£103,000) is very close to median state pension wealth (£99,000), indicating that there are not many extreme values inflating the mean. Also, the ratio between the 75th percentile and the 25th percentile is only 1.8. In contrast, mean private pension wealth (£189,000) is far higher than median private pension wealth (£109,000) and the ratio between the 75th and 25th percentiles is 16.0.

It is not surprising that private pension wealth is more unevenly distributed than state pension wealth. Virtually everyone in the age group will have some entitlement to state pension income in retirement, from those who simply have entitlement to the basic state pension (BSP) on the basis of their partner's contributions to those having accrued entitlement to both the BSP and the second-tier state pension (SERPS/S2P) on the basis of their own employment and earnings history. Furthermore, the maximum entitlement to state pension income is limited by having accrued full entitlement to the BSP and the fact that SERPS/S2P entitlement is only accrued on earnings up to the upper earnings limit. This is compounded by the fact that higher-earning individuals have been more likely to be contracted out of SERPS than lower-earning individuals.[2] Therefore the range of state pension entitlements that individuals can have is naturally limited. In contrast, we expect the distribution of private pension wealth to be unequal because, as is discussed in Section 3.2, one-in-four individuals have never been members of private pension plans (and so have no entitlement) whilst some have accrued large entitlements to private pensions through many years of membership and high earnings during those years.

The last row of Table 3.1 shows that the combined effect of highly unequally distributed private pension wealth and more evenly distributed state pension wealth is that total pension wealth is unevenly distributed, though less so than private pension wealth. The ratio of the 75th percentile to the 25th percentile is 3.2. Nearly a quarter of individuals have pension wealth of less than £120,000, whilst a quarter have pension wealth in excess of £380,000. At an annuity rate of 5 per cent, these levels of wealth would provide an annual income of approximately £6,000 and £19,000 respectively.

The figures in Table 3.1, however, mask the fact that pension wealth varies significantly by family type and, to a lesser extent, age. This is in part because of

---

[2] See table 5.1 of Department for Work and Pensions, Second Tier Pension Statistics, http://www.dwp.gov.uk/asd/asd1/dsu/second_tier/2002_03/STPP_Tables_2002_03.xls.

Table 3.2
Mean and median pension wealth by family type and age (£000s)

	Age				Unweighted N
	50–54	**55–59**	**60–64**	*All*	
Single people	132.0	145.9	165.8	*143.0*	999
	(74.7)	(91.4)	(116.6)	*(89.8)*	
Of which:					
Single men	135.0	144.8	165.8	*147.5*	470
	(76.8)	(87.6)	(116.6)	*(96.2)*	
Single women	129.8	146.8	n/a	*137.8*	529
	(73.6)	(94.7)	(n/a)	*(81.3)*	
Couples	317.2	337.9	354.7	*331.9*	3,688
	(237.1)	(265.9)	(274.6)	*(257.8)*	
All	*277.8*	*296.8*	*318.1*	*292.2*	*4,687*
	(200.9)	*(225.7)*	*(242.4)*	*(219.3)*	

Notes: Medians are shown in parentheses. One observation per individual aged between 50 and the SPA.

the measure of pension wealth used – namely, current family pension wealth. This produces variations in pension wealth by family type and age for two reasons. First, because the definition of pension wealth used here is measured at the family level, individuals in couples on average have higher total pension wealth than single people. However, this does not necessarily mean that couples are better off than single people, because unless there are complete returns to scale in families, a couple will also need higher levels of wealth to enjoy the same retirement consumption as a single person. Second, because current pension wealth is used, younger individuals will have had fewer years during which to accrue pension wealth than older individuals, so they may appear less wealthy. Table 3.2 shows mean and median levels of pension wealth by family type and age. Mean pension wealth is shown in the top line of each row, with the median shown below it in parentheses.

Table 3.2 shows that median pension wealth of single people is just £90,000, less than half that of individuals in couples (for whom median pension wealth is £258,000). It also shows that even the wealthiest group of single people (men aged 60–64) do not have median pension wealth anywhere close to median pension wealth for the whole sample (£219,000) – median pension wealth amongst single men aged 60–64 is just £117,000. Average wealth amongst individuals in couples is at least twice as great as average wealth amongst single individuals of the same age. Since the consumption needs of couples are unlikely to be more than twice as high as those of single people in retirement, couples will on average be able to fund a higher level of retirement consumption than single people.

Pension wealth is also slightly higher amongst older individuals – median pension wealth of individuals aged between 50 and 54 is £201,000, compared with £226,000 for individuals aged between 55 and 59.[3] This pattern remains true for each family type as well. Single men aged 60–64 have £40,000 more pension

---

[3] As we include here only those individuals aged between 50 and the SPA, it is worth remembering that the 60–64 age group will only contain men (or couples where the oldest partner aged between 50 and the SPA is a man aged between 60 and 64).

Figure 3.1
Cumulative distribution of total family pension wealth (all families aged 50–
SPA, by five-year age band)

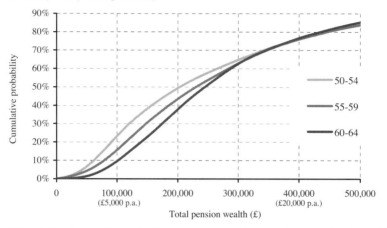

Notes: Number of observations = 4,687. One observation per individual aged between 50 and the SPA. The density functions are estimated using an Epanechnikov kernel with a band width of £20,000.

wealth at the median than single men aged 50–54. These age differences could either reflect the fact that older individuals have had longer to accrue wealth or reflect differences between the cohorts, or a combination of both. There are not major differences, however, between single men and single women – single women aged 50–54 have about the same level of pension wealth at the median (£74,000) as single men of the same age (£77,000).

The cumulative distribution of total pension wealth, again measured at the family level, is shown by age band in Figure 3.1. This shows that, for example, 49 per cent of those aged 50–54 have less than £200,000 of current pension wealth, compared with 44 per cent of those aged 55–59 and 38 per cent of those aged 60–64.

In Tables 3.1 and 3.2 and throughout this chapter, we look at pension wealth at the family level. The reason for focusing on this rather than individual pension wealth is that family pension wealth is likely to provide a better indication of the resources available to individuals to fund their retirement consumption; looking solely at individual pension wealth ignores the fact that many couples will share (at least some of) their pension income. However, it is still of interest to know what proportion of a couple's pension wealth each partner holds in their own right. This, for example, gives some indication of the minimum wealth that the less wealthy partner would be left with in the event of partnership dissolution and no subsequent pension sharing. Therefore Table 3.3 shows the mean and median proportion of couples' pension wealth that is held by men and by women. Because individuals do not always form partnerships with someone of the same age, the means for men and women do not sum to 100 per cent in the table. Across all age groups, men hold a

Table 3.3
Percentage of family pension wealth held by each individual in a couple (mean and median, by gender and age, all individuals in couples aged 50–SPA)

	Age				Unweighted N
	50–54	**55–59**	**60–64**	***All***	
Men	64.5 (66.8)	63.9 (66.7)	68.5 (71.3)	*65.4 (68.2)*	2,156
Women	38.3 (36.8)	36.8 (34.0)	n/a (n/a)	*37.5 (35.6)*	1,532

Notes: Medians are shown in parentheses. One observation per individual in a couple who is aged between 50 and the SPA.

higher proportion of couples' pension wealth than women. In all age groups, men on average hold approximately 60–70 per cent of household pension wealth and women hold approximately 30–40 per cent. So, in general, women in couples hold less than half of their family's pension wealth. Whilst on average they hold less pension wealth in their own right than their partner, women in couples do still hold a significant part of their family's pension wealth.

3.2 Composition of pension wealth

The pension wealth described in Tables 3.1 and 3.2 comes from various sources – state pensions, (current and past) employer-provided defined benefit (DB) plans, (current and past) employer-provided defined contribution (DC) plans and (current and past) personal and stakeholder pensions. This section provides more details on the composition of pension wealth, focusing on the different forms in which private pension wealth can be held. This is important because different types of pension wealth will vary in terms of the formal risks faced by individuals and the likely future accrual. In particular, pension wealth held in (current or past) DB pension plans might be less exposed to investment and annuity rate risk than wealth held in DC pension plans.[4] Furthermore, future accrual is likely to be higher for wealth held in DC pension plans than in (current or past) DB plans.[5]

Table 3.4 provides summary statistics on the pension arrangements of those aged between 50 and the SPA. It shows that half of the sample (50.1 per cent) are currently a member of a private pension plan and that a quarter (24.3 per cent) have never been a member of a private pension. Men are more likely to be a member of a current pension plan, and less likely to have never been a member of a private pension plan, than women. Relatively strong cohort effects can be seen, with younger individuals being less likely to have never joined a private pension: for

---

[4] People in DB pension plans could still be exposed to some investment risk and annuity rate risk since, for example, their future wage growth might in part depend on the cost of their employer's pension contributions. Moreover, *private sector* DB plans could fail, although this risk will have been mitigated, at least to some extent, by the new Pension Protection Fund (PPF).

[5] For a discussion of the economic consequences of a shift from DB to DC pensions, see Banks, Blundell and Emmerson (2005).

Table 3.4

Percentage of individuals with current membership of DB and DC pensions, past pensions[a] only and no private pension at all (all aged 50–SPA)

	Men				Women			*All*
	50–54	55–59	60–64	*All*	50–54	55–59	*All*	
Has current pension	67.9	55.6	33.4	*53.8*	50.7	38.5	*44.8*	*50.1*
Of which:								
DB only	27.3	18.9	8.3	*19.0*	24.5	17.3	*21.0*	*19.8*
DC only	36.8	33.8	21.8	*31.5*	20.5	15.6	*18.1*	*26.0*
DB + DC	2.6	1.3	1.2	*1.8*	1.8	1.5	*1.6*	*1.7*
Don't know	1.1	1.5	2.0	*1.5*	3.8	4.1	*4.0*	*2.5*
No current pension	32.1	44.4	66.6	*46.2*	49.3	61.5	*55.2*	*49.9*
Of which:								
Any past pension not in receipt	11.5	11.6	8.9	*10.8*	9.4	10.4	*9.9*	*10.4*
All past pensions in receipt	8.1	17.6	41.5	*20.9*	3.0	11.3	*7.0*	*15.2*
No private pension	12.4	15.1	16.1	*14.4*	37.0	39.8	*38.4*	*24.3*
Sample size	*971*	*906*	*749*	*2,626*	*1,061*	*1,000*	*2,061*	*4,687*

[a] Throughout this chapter, past pensions (both those in receipt and those not in receipt) include entitlements to pensions inherited from deceased or divorced former partners.
Note: One observation per individual aged between 50 and the SPA.

example, 37.0 per cent of women aged 50–54 have never been a member of a private pension plan compared with 39.8 per cent of women aged 55–59. Also shown in Table 3.4 is the proportion of individuals who report being a member of a current DB or a current DC pension plan. A higher proportion of men aged between 50 and the SPA are a member of a DC plan than of a DB plan, whereas the converse is true for women.

Figure 3.2 decomposes the skewed distribution of pension wealth into each of its constituent parts. Mean pension wealth amongst the wealthiest 10 per cent of individuals is about £874,000, whereas the poorest 10 per cent of individuals have mean pension wealth of just £48,000. These large differences in wealth are principally driven by wealthier individuals having large amounts of wealth from current DB plans and also from plans from which they are already receiving a pension (which could have been DB or DC plans). Table 3.5 shows that 70.7 per cent of individuals in the wealthiest decile group have a current DB pension, while just over half (50.7 per cent) are already receiving income from a private pension. Whilst even those in the 5th decile have virtually no wealth from these two sources (although 25.1 per cent of individuals have a DB pension and 31.0 per cent are receiving income from a private pension, mean wealth is just £25,000 in current DB plans and £21,000 from past pensions in receipt for the 5th decile), individuals in the 9th decile have mean wealth of £203,000 from current DB plans and £134,000 from past pensions in receipt (and the figures are even greater for the 10th decile).

Amongst those with the least pension wealth, state pensions are, of course, a very important part of total pension wealth – state pensions account for at least 70

Figure 3.2
Mean family pension wealth in each form by decile of total pension wealth

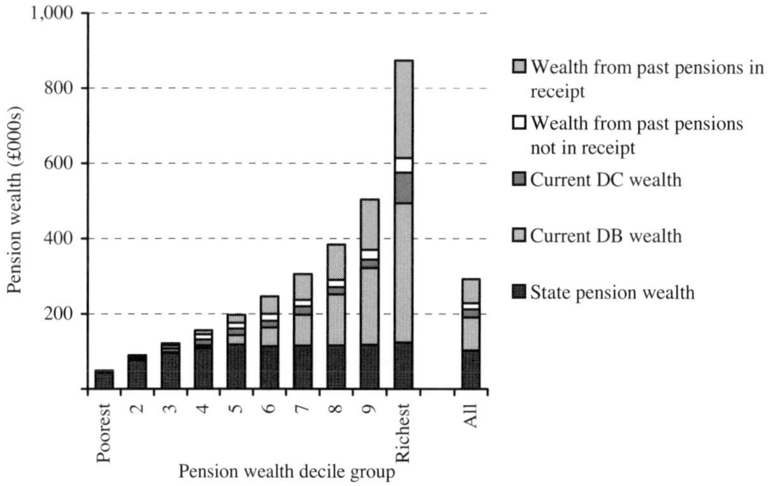

Notes: The very wealthiest individuals (approximately 1 per cent of the sample) have extremely high levels of pension wealth. As a result, the mean levels of pension wealth shown for the richest decile are increased by a relatively small number of individuals within this group. However, even excluding the wealthiest 1 per cent does not change the overall picture of how wealth is held by wealthy individuals. Therefore all individuals are included. Sample size = 4,687. One observation per individual aged between 50 and the SPA. Details of decile cut points can be found in Table 4.1.

Table 3.5
Percentage of individuals in each decile holding pension wealth in each form

Pension wealth decile group	State	DB	DC	Past pension yet to draw	Past pension in receipt	Unweighted N
Poorest	85.8	0.9	21.9	15.0	4.4	460
2	98.5	2.5	39.2	25.9	9.2	448
3	98.9	3.4	54.0	27.2	14.1	461
4	98.9	10.1	58.3	33.5	21.6	464
5	98.8	25.1	52.0	35.6	31.0	473
6	99.4	35.5	42.6	31.8	40.0	472
7	99.0	45.5	45.1	31.5	44.0	480
8	99.5	57.9	39.7	32.1	45.7	474
9	99.9	64.7	36.7	33.4	47.6	476
Richest	99.7	70.7	36.3	30.5	50.7	479
All	*97.8*	*31.6*	*42.6*	*29.6*	*30.8*	*4,687*

Notes: One observation per individual aged between 50 and the SPA. Details of decile cut points can be found in Table 4.1.

Figure 3.3
Mean family pension wealth in each form by decile of total family pension
wealth, as pension portfolio shares

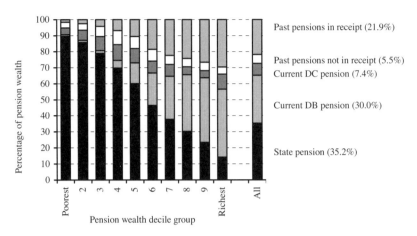

Past pensions in receipt (21.9%)

Past pensions not in receipt (5.5%)
Current DC pension (7.4%)

Current DB pension (30.0%)

State pension (35.2%)

Note: See Notes to Figure 3.2.

per cent of total pension wealth for each of the bottom three deciles. This is
highlighted in Figure 3.3, which presents the same information as Figure 3.2 but
with each component of pension wealth shown as a share of total pension wealth.
Figure 3.3 shows that individuals, on average, hold 35.2 per cent of pension wealth
in state pensions, 30.0 per cent in current DB schemes, 7.4 per cent in current DC
schemes, 5.5 per cent in past pensions from which they do not currently receive any
income and the remaining 21.9 per cent in pensions from which they are already
receiving an income.

Because state pension wealth does not increase very much across the pension
wealth deciles (mean state pension wealth is just £124,000 amongst individuals in
the richest decile, compared with £109,000 amongst individuals in the 4th decile), it
is an increasingly less significant component of total pension wealth amongst the
individuals in the top deciles of the pension wealth distribution. Individuals in the
top deciles of pension wealth have large amounts of wealth in current DB plans –
wealth from such plans accounts for over 30 per cent of total pension wealth
amongst the top three deciles. Similarly, the wealthiest deciles are also already
drawing pensions from previous plans (at least 40 per cent of individuals in the top
five decile groups are already receiving income from a private pension, whereas less
than 10 per cent of individuals in the poorest two deciles are – see Table 3.5) – at
least 20 per cent of pension wealth for the wealthiest 40 per cent of individuals
comes from pensions from which they are already receiving an income.

From these figures, it appears that a lot of wealth is derived from current DB
plans, with far less coming from current DC plans. Wealth from current DC
pensions is most important for individuals in the 3rd, 4th and 5th deciles, where (as
Table 3.5 shows) just over half of individuals have a current DC pension. However,

18

wealth from current DC pensions does not constitute more than 10 per cent of total pension wealth for any group. This should not be interpreted as necessarily showing that DB plans are more generous than DC plans. Rather, this finding is, at least in part, due to two factors. First, the age group we are focusing on here is all individuals aged between 50 and the state pension age. If we were to look at younger individuals, we would probably find that current DC pension wealth is more important, as younger individuals will have been more significantly affected by the shift from DB to DC plans that has occurred since 1988. Second, those individuals who belong to DB plans tend to be higher earners than those who belong to DC plans or to no pension plan at all. In other words, those people with high current DB wealth are people we would expect to have high levels of pension wealth anyway, because they are high earners. Figure 3.4 shows the distribution of earnings for individuals with different current pension types. Individuals who are currently members of DB plans have median earnings of £280 a week, compared with £240 a week for individuals who are currently members of DC plans and just £150 a week for individuals who are not currently members of a private pension plan.

The final category of wealth is wealth from pensions that individuals are no longer members of but from which they are not yet drawing a pension. Figure 3.3 shows that wealth in such a form makes up only a small proportion of total pension wealth for all groups. The individuals with the greatest amount of wealth in past plans are those in the 10th decile, who on average have £38,000 of wealth in past pensions from which they are not yet drawing an income. However, this is just 4.4 per cent of mean total pension wealth for this decile. This is not surprising given that only 47.3 per cent of individuals report being a member of any past pension

Figure 3.4
Distribution of current earnings by current pension status

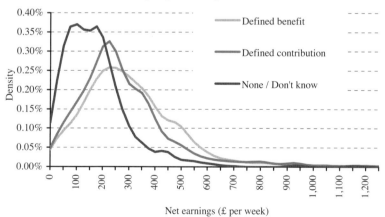

Net earnings (£ per week)

Notes: Current pension status is defined based on the pension type of the most important current pension of which an individual is a member. One observation per employed/self-employed individual.
Source: Banks, Emmerson and Oldfield, 2005.

plans and that the median tenure in current pension plans is 13 years (Banks, Emmerson and Oldfield, 2005).

The overall picture that emerges is that the individuals with the lowest pension wealth are those who are relying almost entirely on state pensions. The importance of state pensions declines across wealthier individuals, with the wealthiest having large amounts of pension wealth in private pensions, in many cases already drawing pensions from such plans before having reached the SPA.

3.3 Association between pension wealth and other characteristics

From a policy perspective, it is important to know which individuals have low levels of pension wealth. Once we can identify the types of people who are likely to have low pension wealth, we can begin to try to understand the reasons behind it. Only then can we begin to design the appropriate policy response (if any). We have already seen that pension wealth varies by age and family type, but there are also many other characteristics by which we would expect pension wealth to vary. For example, we might expect different levels of pension wealth amongst people with different current employment statuses.[6] Table 3.6 shows the distribution of family pension wealth by employment status – this is shown separately for couples and single people because the definition of being 'in work' that is used differs between couples and singles.

The top half of Table 3.6 shows that, on average, individuals in couples in which both partners are in paid work have about the same level of pension wealth as

Table 3.6
Distribution of total family pension wealth by employment status (all families aged 50–SPA, £000s)

	Mean	p25	Median	p75	Unweighted N
Couples	*331.9*	*152.8*	*257.8*	*426.7*	*3,688*
Neither in paid work, not both retired	244.3	118.7	182.8	313.0	444
Both retired	571.9	278.7	384.9	659.5	168
One partner in paid work	338.3	156.8	260.7	424.2	1,066
Both in paid work	328.8	157.5	260.2	437.9	2,010
Single people	*143.0*	*58.8*	*89.8*	*187.0*	*999*
In paid work	161.5	62.5	104.1	218.3	598
Retired	208.3	96.2	176.3	283.5	112
Other inactive	80.1	48.4	65.9	91.4	289
All	*292.2*	*120.3*	*219.3*	*380.0*	*4,687*

Note: One observation per individual aged between 50 and the SPA.

---

[6] Note that in addition to current employment status, employment history is likely to be as (if not more) important in terms of its variation with pension wealth. Although not available in the first two waves of ELSA, wave 3 (2006–07) will collect full employment history via a life history interview.

Figure 3.5
Mean, 25th percentile point, median and 75th percentile point of total family pension wealth by current income decile

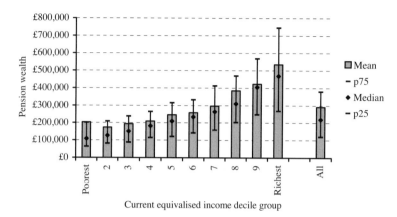

Notes: Sample size = 4,687. One observation per individual aged between 50 and the SPA.

individuals in couples where just one partner is in paid work (median wealth of £260,000 compared with £261,000). However, individuals in couples where neither member is in paid work and both report that they are retired have, on average, the highest levels of pension wealth, with median pension wealth of £385,000. In contrast, individuals in couples where neither member is in paid work and at least one of them does not report themselves as retired have, on average, the lowest levels of pension wealth (median pension wealth among this group is £183,000). This highlights the extent to which those aged between 50 and the SPA who are not in paid work comprise both the rich (who tend to choose to retire early) and the poor (who tend to move out of work due to limited labour market opportunities). The bottom half of Table 3.6 shows that the same is true for single people – the highest average level of pension wealth is seen among those not in paid work and retired, while the lowest average level is seen among those who are not in paid work but report not being retired.

We would also expect pension wealth to vary by current income. Most pensions are in some way earnings related: for those contracted in, second-tier state pension entitlement tends to rise with earnings; income from DB plans is calculated typically on some measure of final salary; and contributions to DC plans are often calculated as a percentage of earnings. Figure 3.5 shows total family pension wealth by current income decile. Those on higher incomes have higher levels of pension wealth, which we would expect if individuals aim to achieve some desired replacement rate in retirement. The 10 per cent of individuals with the highest current incomes have median pension wealth of £469,000, whereas the 10 per cent of individuals with the lowest incomes have median pension wealth of just £109,000.

Inequality expressed as the absolute difference between the 25th and 75th percentile points changes as current income increases and is greatest in the top decile – the wealthiest 25 per cent of individuals in this current income decile have at least £477,000 more pension wealth than the poorest 25 per cent of individuals in this current income decile. The proportionate difference between the wealthiest and least wealthy in each current income decile is about the same (and quite large) across all the decile groups. The ratio between the 75th and 25th percentiles is 3.2 in the bottom income decile, 2.6 in the 5th decile and 2.8 in the richest decile. So, whilst it is generally true that higher-income individuals have higher levels of pension wealth, there is still great inequality in wealth even amongst those with similar current incomes.

The variation in current pension wealth among individuals with similar current incomes could be due to some having current income that was not a particularly good summary of their lifetime income (particularly since the decision to retire (and hence about having earnings) is a matter of choice for many of those aged between 50 and the SPA). In the absence of a lifetime income measure, Figure 3.6 shows total family pension wealth by decile of gross housing wealth, since this might better reflect lifetime resources. Comparison of this graph and Figure 3.5 shows that at least some of the very acute variation in pension wealth across the income distribution is due to the use of current income deciles (which in turn depend heavily on earnings), although, if anything, the spread of pension wealth within each housing wealth group is greater. This suggests that individuals with similar lifetime incomes have chosen to save different amounts in pensions, potentially with offsetting amounts saved in other forms – an issue that is explored in detail in Chapter 4.

Figure 3.6
Mean, 25th percentile point, median and 75th percentile point of total family pension wealth by gross housing wealth decile

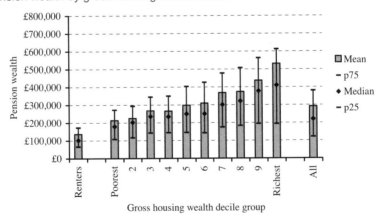

Notes: Sample size = 4,687. One observation per individual aged between 50 and the SPA. Renters are excluded from the gross housing wealth deciles.

The tables and graphs presented so far in this chapter have suggested some factors that may be correlated with the level of pension wealth (such as employment status and family type). However, these factors could simply be acting as a proxy for other underlying characteristics associated with both pension wealth and these other factors. Table 3.7 presents the results of a multivariate analysis of pension wealth. Total family pension wealth is regressed on various individual characteristics – family non-pension current income, education level, gender, family type, employment status, health status and age. The results from three quantile regressions (for the 25th, 50th and 75th percentiles) are shown. We use non-pension income here because, for those individuals who are already in receipt of pensions, current pension income and pension wealth will, by definition, be highly correlated.[7]

Table 3.7
Multivariate analysis of total family pension wealth

	Pension wealth (£000s)					
	Quantile					
	25th percentile		50th percentile		75th percentile	
	Coeff.	S.E.	Coeff.	S.E.	Coeff.	S.E.
Non-pension income decile						
2	−9.45	6.50	−30.37	8.73	−49.80	15.07
3	−20.95	7.06	−39.13	9.29	−51.12	16.24
4	−14.67	6.78	−23.20	9.60	−28.39	17.59
5	−14.69	7.36	−39.27	10.11	−41.14	18.40
6	−3.62	7.50	−16.13	10.11	−31.11	19.16
7	3.84	7.23	1.70	12.38	12.18	18.22
8	11.10	8.94	33.62	16.53	74.31	21.03
9	54.35	13.49	71.13	20.46	103.66	22.02
Richest	81.39	14.99	162.72	26.87	228.99	31.71
No formal qualifications	−19.09	3.38	−35.59	5.30	−77.79	9.00
Degree	40.32	6.29	102.92	9.60	128.50	15.02
Single male	−70.91	4.15	−102.37	6.84	−161.76	10.01
Single female	−67.67	6.61	−88.03	7.41	−144.15	11.18
Couple female	23.48	4.38	37.17	7.36	35.17	10.30
Not in paid work	−12.21	6.18	−16.17	8.75	16.70	16.33
Health problems	−12.12	3.89	−17.33	5.89	−43.38	8.31
Age − 50	6.28	0.72	5.98	0.87	5.33	1.56
(Not in paid work) × (Age − 50)	0.79	1.01	2.81	1.30	2.59	2.46
Constant	117.10	7.30	198.94	12.10	346.59	18.90

Notes: The omitted group is 50-year-old men in couples in the bottom decile of current income, who have A levels, are in paid work and report no health problems. Non-pension income is total family unequivalised income from all sources other than pensions. Dependent variable is total family pension wealth; independent variables are individual characteristics. Sample size = 4,687 observations. One observation per individual aged between 50 and the SPA. Standard errors are estimated by bootstrapping with 100 repetitions.

---

[7] Note, however, that any measurement error in current earnings will be positively correlated with predicted wealth in DB schemes, as current earnings are used to estimate the final salary on which DB schemes are based.

The implication of using non-pension income as an explanatory variable is that those individuals whose only current source of income is private pensions will appear in the bottom decile of non-pension income. However, these individuals will actually have relatively high pension wealth. It is for this reason that we find that those in current income deciles 2 to 6 have lower wealth on average than the poorest income group (i.e. we observe negative and, in most cases, statistically significant coefficients on deciles 2 to 6 of current income). Having current income in the top 30 per cent of the income distribution, however, is significantly positively correlated with pension wealth. An individual in the top 10 per cent of the income distribution will have pension wealth at the median £163,000 higher than an otherwise identical individual in the bottom 10 per cent of the income distribution.

Conditional on current income, not being in paid work is associated with lower pension wealth at the 25th percentile and at the median but higher pension wealth at the 75th percentile (although the coefficient at the 75th percentile is not significantly different from zero at conventional statistical levels). This is consistent with those out of work being the 'retired', who are relatively rich on average, and those with limited labour market opportunities (perhaps due to poor health), who are relatively poor on average.

Even conditional on current income and employment status, we find that education level is significantly associated with pension wealth. An individual with no qualifications has pension wealth that is £36,000 lower at the median than an otherwise identical individual who has qualifications up to A level or equivalent. Similarly, having a degree (rather than having non-degree-level qualifications) is associated with £103,000 of additional pension wealth at the median.

Conditional on all the other characteristics, women have higher pension wealth than men. Women in couples (all other things being equal) have £37,000 more pension wealth at the median than men in couples. While single women have £88,000 less pension wealth at the median than men in couples, single men have £102,000 less pension wealth at the median than men in couples. In part, this will be because, on average, women will receive their state pensions and final salary pensions for longer, due to their longer life expectancy and to the fact that, for the majority of the women in this sample, their state pension age is lower than the male state pension age.[8] Therefore women will have higher state pension wealth than men even if they have identical earnings and employment histories. Even though women have slightly higher pension wealth on average than men, because of their longer life expectancies, this wealth will need to be consumed over more years, on average. Therefore annual income in retirement may not be higher for women than for men, as annuity rates available to men are typically higher than those available to women.

As we would expect, individuals who report health problems that limit their daily activities have significantly lower pension wealth at each of the quartiles than individuals who do not report limiting health problems (at the median, individuals with health problems have £17,000 less pension wealth than those without). This relationship is discussed in more detail in Section 4.4.

Older individuals have higher levels of pension wealth than younger individuals, again as we would expect. Older individuals have had more years to accumulate

---

[8] The female SPA is currently 60. It is set to be increased by 1 month every 2 months between 2010 and 2020, to become equal to the male SPA.

pension wealth and so would be expected to have higher levels than otherwise identical younger individuals. Each year that an individual is aged over 50 is associated with £6,000 of additional pension wealth (at the median for an individual in paid work).

3.4 Pension replacement rates

All of the analysis in this chapter so far has looked at the level of pension wealth held by families. However, the current debate on pensions tends to focus on fears that pension saving will be 'inadequate'. Attempting to define adequacy clearly raises the question: 'adequate for what?'. Changes in state payments to pensioners in recent years (such as increased targeted support and attempts to increase the take-up of means-tested benefits)[9] have been focused on ensuring pensioners have incomes that are adequate for avoidance of income poverty. However, most people would probably wish to achieve savings that are adequate to maintain something comparable to the standard of living that they had prior to retirement (i.e. adequacy measured by some desired replacement rate, which could vary by income level). The level of saving required to achieve a given replacement rate will be higher for households that have high pre-retirement income.

This section looks at what proportion of current family income will be replaced by pension income when individuals reach the SPA for families where at least one member is currently in paid work. We focus on those currently in paid work because for individuals who are retired and already drawing income from private pensions, pension replacement rates will generally be at least 100 per cent. The replacement rates here do not include retirement income from any sources other than state and private pensions. (Chapter 6 looks in more detail at the extent to which individuals' total retirement resources, including potential receipt of the

Table 3.8
Pension replacement rates (ratio of net pension income at the SPA to total net income in 2002, assuming immediate retirement)

	Replacement rate (%)			% with replacement rate in range:			Unweighted N
	p25	Median	p75	0–50%	51–66%	67%+	
Men	*48.6*	*67.1*	*91.6*	*26.8*	*23.2*	*50.1*	*1,945*
50–54	46.3	61.8	84.8	31.9	25.3	42.8	729
55–59	49.6	68.2	92.8	25.2	23.4	51.5	776
60–64	56.3	75.3	102.8	19.3	18.5	62.2	440
Women	*48.9*	*67.5*	*92.2*	*26.1*	*23.2*	*50.7*	*1,594*
50–54	47.2	63.9	86.2	28.8	26.3	45.0	819
55–59	51.5	74.5	96.2	22.9	19.3	57.8	775
All	*48.8*	*67.4*	*91.8*	*26.5*	*23.2*	*50.3*	*3,539*

Notes: These figures only include single people who are currently in paid work and couples where at least one member is in paid work. One observation per employed/self-employed individual aged between 50 and the SPA.

---

[9] For a discussion of recent policy trends, see, for example, Clark and Emmerson (2003).

pension credit, will replace current income.) Table 3.8 provides figures on the distribution of 'pension replacement rates' for those currently in paid work. Here, we define the pension replacement rate as total net family pension income that will be received at the SPA as a percentage of current net family income. Pension income is calculated on the basis that everyone retires immediately and that no further state or private pension wealth is accumulated. Of course, at least some of these individuals (particularly the younger ones) will continue accruing additional pension rights beyond 2002 and so (ignoring future changes in income) will actually achieve higher replacement rates at the SPA than Table 3.8 suggests. Moreover, in retirement, many individuals will not be solely reliant on their pension income, as a result of having non-pension wealth or entitlement to the means-tested pension credit. These broader issues will be examined in more detail in Chapter 6.

In terms of the simple 'pension replacement rate', we find that older individuals have higher replacement rates than younger ones. This may reflect two factors. First, older individuals have had longer to build up their pension wealth and so will have higher income in retirement. Second, older individuals may be more likely than younger individuals to have moved into part-time work as they approach retirement and so their current income may be lower than it was earlier in their working life; thus their replacement rates are higher than those for younger groups, even if (for example) the ratio between their retirement income and their income at age 50 is the same as for those individuals currently aged 50.

Over half of all working individuals aged under, but within five years of, the SPA have current pension wealth that would provide them with a net replacement rate of at least 67 per cent. This might be a useful benchmark, as the 2002 DWP Green Paper states that 'current pensioners have, on average, an income that is equal to two-thirds of average earnings of working-age people just before retirement'.[10] There is also a fairly significant group of individuals whose current pension entitlements would provide them with replacement of 50 per cent or less of their current income. Based on their current pension entitlements alone, 19.3 per cent of 60- to 64-year-old men and 22.9 per cent of 55- to 59-year-old women have pension replacement rates of 50 per cent or less.

---

[10] Source: Paragraph 48, page 27 of Department for Work and Pensions (2002). In fact, annex 4 (paragraph 3, page 151) of the Green Paper states that this replacement rate of 63 per cent is calculated by taking those aged within five years either side of the SPA and comparing the incomes of people who consider themselves retired and those of people still in paid work. Given that, as we have shown in Table 3.6, those who report themselves as being retired are relatively rich, this measure is likely to overstate replacement rates.

CHAPTER 4
The Correlation of Pension Wealth and Other Sources of Wealth

The previous chapter showed that, whilst there are some families with very high levels of pension wealth, there are others with very low levels of pension wealth – 25 per cent of individuals are in families that have pension wealth that would generate incomes of less than £6,000 per year. However, families may hold other assets that they could use to fund their consumption in retirement. For example, families could use financial wealth, business and property wealth (particularly in the case of self-employed individuals who may have large business assets) or owner-occupied housing wealth to fund their retirement consumption. Assuming individuals use housing wealth to fund retirement consumption is rather controversial (as housing has both consumption and investment value), although some fraction of housing wealth can certainly be released by, for example, downsizing the home or through a home reversion plan.

This chapter examines the extent to which other forms of assets might substitute for pension wealth and documents the distribution of total wealth amongst the cohort of individuals currently approaching the state pension age (SPA). Section 4.1 provides a description of the distribution of total wealth. As was the case in Chapter 3, throughout this chapter wealth figures refer to family-level wealth. Section 4.2 looks at the correlation between pension and non-pension wealth. In Section 4.3, we turn to look at the composition of total wealth. Section 4.4 looks at the relationship between total wealth and other individual characteristics such as current health and also describes the extent to which individuals with certain characteristics are located in different parts of the overall wealth distribution.

4.1   Distribution of total wealth

Previous work has shown that the distribution of other forms of wealth (particularly financial wealth) is very unequal, as Chapter 3 found is so for the distribution of private pension wealth. For example, Banks, Karlsen and Oldfield (2003) demonstrated that although mean financial wealth amongst the population aged 50 and over is over £40,000, a quarter of this population have less than £1,500. Table 4.1 shows the distribution of each form of wealth and of total wealth across all families with at least one member aged between 50 and the SPA. There is a lot of variation in the amounts of wealth that families hold in each of these assets but the inequality in the distribution of wealth is greater for some assets than for others.

The first three rows of Table 4.1 show the distribution of pension wealth, which was described in more detail in Chapter 3. The next three rows show the distribution of other forms of wealth that people could also easily use to fund retirement consumption. These are financial wealth and business and property wealth. The

Table 4.1
Deciles of each form of wealth (£000s)

	p10	p20	p30	p40	p50	p60	p70	p80	p90
Total pension wealth	73.1	105.5	138.5	175.8	219.3	276.8	342.5	433.3	583.3
Composed of:									
State pension wealth	50.5	65.9	77.6	88.1	98.6	109.1	121.9	139.3	164.5
Private pension wealth	0	8.5	25.9	60.0	109.4	161.4	229.9	320.1	473.7
Other wealth	−0.8	0.5	4.0	11.5	22.5	39.1	65.3	109.0	221.2
Composed of:									
Financial wealth	−1.7	0.1	2.2	6.7	14.8	24.4	40.2	65.0	111.6
Business and property wealth	0	0	0	0	0	0	1.1	20.0	110.0
Housing wealth	0	18.0	57.0	80.0	101.0	130.0	160.0	200.0	290.0
Total non-pension wealth	*0.3*	*37.0*	*76.6*	*108.1*	*142.0*	*184.3*	*236.4*	*320.3*	*477.6*
Total wealth	*108.0*	*189.9*	*260.9*	*321.3*	*394.6*	*485.5*	*595.6*	*736.9*	*1,003.7*

Notes: Housing wealth is owner-occupied housing wealth net of any outstanding mortgage. The columns of the table do not sum as the deciles are defined over each form of wealth separately, rather than being the deciles of total wealth. In other words, different individuals appear in the bottom decile of state pension wealth and in the bottom decile of financial wealth (for example). Sample size = 4,687. One observation per individual aged between 50 and the SPA.

table also shows the distributions of housing wealth, non-pension wealth and total wealth.

At least 10 per cent of individuals have negative net financial wealth (i.e. they have net debts) – at the 10th percentile, net family financial wealth is –£1,700. Since only just over 30 per cent of individuals have any business and property wealth, at least 10 per cent of families have net debts even when we take into account this other wealth (£800 of debt at the 10th percentile). However, a few families have very high levels of wealth held in these forms, with 20 per cent of individuals having at least £109,000 of wealth in financial and business assets and (non-owner-occupied) property, which could be used to fund consumption during retirement.

At least some housing wealth could probably be used to fund retirement consumption, although (as mentioned above) the extent to which individuals might use this wealth to fund consumption in retirement is less certain. Individuals will still need somewhere to live during retirement, so they would not be able to liquidate their entire housing wealth without having to pay for rented accommodation. However, many families may be able to downsize and thus release some of the equity in their house for consumption, or release equity in some other way such as through a home reversion plan. Of course, some individuals may have earmarked their houses to bequeath on their death. However, these individuals should not be considered any differently from individuals who intend to bequeath non-housing assets or those who do not wish to make a bequest but have other consumption needs in retirement. Table 4.1 shows that at least 80 per cent of individuals aged between 50 and the SPA have some net housing wealth. Half of individuals have at least £101,000 of net housing wealth, while 20 per cent have at least £200,000, some (though probably not all) of which could be used to fund consumption in retirement.

The last row of Table 4.1 shows the distribution of total wealth (including housing wealth) across all individuals. This wealth is very unevenly distributed. Individuals at the 80th percentile have 3.9 times as much total wealth as individuals at the 20th percentile of the total wealth distribution. This is the net result of some forms of wealth being more unevenly distributed than others. State pension wealth is the most evenly distributed – individuals at the 80th percentile have only just over twice as much state pension wealth as individuals at the 20th percentile of the state pension wealth distribution. As was mentioned in Chapter 3, given the state pension rules, this relatively equal distribution is not surprising. At the other extreme, financial and physical wealth is the most unevenly distributed – individuals at the 80th percentile have over 200 times as much 'other wealth' as individuals at the 20th percentile of the 'other wealth' distribution.

Though non-pension wealth is very unevenly distributed, most families do hold some non-pension assets. Median total family wealth (£395,000) is significantly higher than median wealth when looking solely at pension wealth (£219,000). So it is clearly important to consider all sources of wealth when assessing whether or not individuals will be able to fund 'adequate' consumption in retirement. Therefore previous analysis that has looked solely at pension wealth or non-pension wealth in isolation will have ignored significant sources of retirement consumption funding for many families.

4.2 Correlation between pension and non-pension wealth

Looking solely at pension or non-pension wealth would be particularly misleading if different forms of assets act as substitutes for one another (i.e. if some families hold high levels of pension wealth but low non-pension wealth, while others hold high non-pension wealth and low pension wealth). Whilst it is possible that other forms of wealth act as substitutes for pension wealth, previous analysis of the ELSA data (Banks, Emmerson and Oldfield, 2005) has suggested that individuals who are currently contributing to a private pension also have higher levels of non-pension wealth.

Figure 4.1, which shows the distribution of pension wealth by decile of non-pension wealth, supports these findings. If pension wealth acted as a substitute for other forms of wealth, we would expect to see a negative gradient of pension wealth across the deciles of non-pension wealth. However, we actually find the opposite result – average pension wealth increases as holdings of other wealth increase. Amongst the 10 per cent of individuals with the most non-pension wealth, median pension wealth is £355,000, compared with just £88,000 for the 10 per cent of families with the least non-pension wealth. In other words, rather than those families with low pension wealth holding high levels of other assets to compensate, at least on average there are simply some wealthy families who hold high levels of all forms of assets and some poor families who hold low levels of all forms of assets. The next section looks at what assets families hold their wealth in and how this varies with the total amount of wealth they have.

Figure 4.1
Distribution of total family pension wealth by decile of total family non-pension wealth

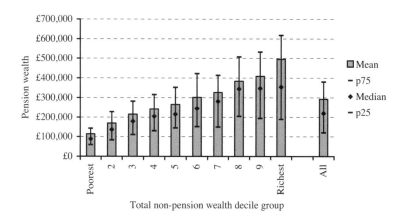

Notes: Sample size = 4,687. One observation per individual aged between 50 and the SPA. Cut points for each decile are provided in Table 4.1.

4.3 Composition of total wealth

Since each form of wealth has different characteristics, it is important to examine the forms that families hold their wealth in and whether this varies across the wealth distribution. As mentioned earlier, housing wealth has some consumption value as well as investment value and so cannot be used for non-housing consumption in its entirety. Pension wealth is principally annuitised. Furthermore, individuals are unable to borrow against their future state pension income, meaning that those with the lowest wealth, who (as we show in this section) hold virtually all their wealth in state pensions, will be unable to reallocate consumption from retirement to the pre-retirement period.[1]

Figure 4.2 shows mean wealth held in each form by decile of total wealth. The wealthiest individuals have, on average, high levels of all forms of private (i.e. non-state-pension) wealth. In contrast, individuals at the bottom of the wealth distribution have low levels of all forms of private wealth. Figure 4.3, which shows the portfolio share of each asset type, demonstrates that the relative importance of each type of asset is different for wealthy and less wealthy groups. On average, individuals hold 19.6 per cent of their total wealth in state pensions, 36.0 per cent in

Figure 4.2
Mean level of each type of wealth by decile of total wealth

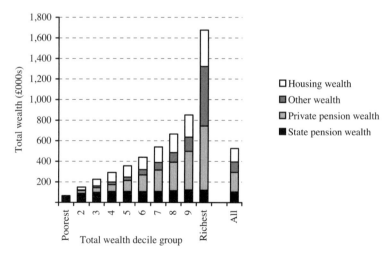

Notes: Sample size = 4,687. One observation per individual aged between 50 and the SPA. Because the richest decile contains some very wealthy individuals, the mean levels of each form of wealth (and particularly financial and physical wealth) are inflated by a small number of extremely wealthy individuals (about the top 1 per cent of the whole distribution). However, excluding these individuals does not dramatically alter the overall picture and so we include all individuals. Cut points for each decile are provided in Table 4.1.

---

[1] While higher-wealth individuals also cannot borrow against their future state pension income, they would be able to run down their non-pension wealth in anticipation of receiving a pension from the state once they reach the SPA.

Figure 4.3
Composition of wealth holdings by decile of total wealth

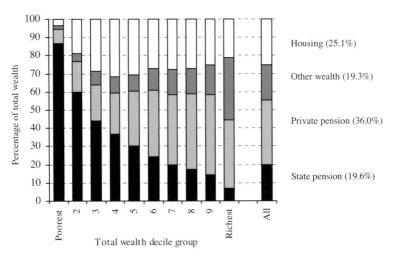

Note: See Notes to Figure 4.2.

private pensions, 25.1 per cent in the form of owner-occupied housing and the remaining 19.3 per cent in other non-pension, non-housing assets. The poorest 10 per cent of individuals are those with virtually no wealth other than state pension wealth. In contrast, state pension wealth accounts for only a very small part of total wealth for the wealthiest because the level of state pension wealth varies comparatively little across individuals.

Mean total family wealth for the poorest 10 per cent of individuals is just £66,000, about £57,000 of which is state pension wealth. State pension wealth does not increase very much on average across the deciles of total wealth, so the relative importance of state pension wealth in the portfolio declines across the wealth deciles. However, as the relative importance of state pension wealth declines, the relative importance of private pension wealth increases. As a result, pension wealth makes up at least 50 per cent of total wealth for individuals in all but the richest decile.

The importance of pension wealth for all individuals is a particularly important finding for the pension adequacy debate because most other studies do not collect accurate information on individuals' (state and private) pension arrangements and so we do not have any other recent evidence of all the resources available to fund retirement consumption. In particular, the relative importance of pension wealth is greater for poorer individuals, whom policymakers are perhaps most likely to be concerned about having inadequate resources. Similarly, analysis that has looked solely at pension wealth will also have ignored a significant part of the resources available to individuals to fund their retirement consumption (particularly for those further up the wealth distribution), as these other forms of wealth make up at least 30 per cent of total wealth for 80 per cent of families.

4.4 Distribution of total wealth by individual characteristics

There are various reasons why families may hold low levels of wealth and the appropriate policy response would depend on which of these applies. First, it may have been suboptimal for some families to have saved any more during their working lives because their incomes during their working lives were also very low. If this were the case, policymakers would probably want to focus on income redistribution either during working lives or in retirement. Second, families may incorrectly believe that their current level of wealth will provide them with more retirement income than it actually will. In this case, policymakers may wish to consider increasing financial education or, on paternalistic grounds, consider increased compulsion. Third, families may have a realistic idea of what income their wealth will provide them with and simply have chosen to accumulate a low level of wealth because they believe this is appropriate. One reason for this is that they might expect to die relatively young. Alternatively, these individuals may have been sensibly responding to the incentives provided to them by the tax, tax credit and benefit system (i.e. the price of retirement consumption was deemed high relative to the price of pre-retirement consumption). To the extent that individuals have better information about their preferences and needs than policymakers, the appropriate policy response in this situation may be to do nothing. Alternatively, policymakers could, for example, decide that the financial incentives provided to individuals to consume before retirement rather than after retirement are not appropriate and should be changed. The extent to which this is an appropriate policy response would depend on the number of individuals affected, their responsiveness to changing the financial incentives that they face and the cost to the taxpayer of doing so.

Therefore, from a policy perspective, it would be useful to be able to characterise which families have low levels of wealth. This will be important for determining whether these low levels of wealth holdings are a problem and, if so, what could be done about it. Table 4.2 shows that, on average, couples have higher levels of wealth than single people, and older individuals generally have higher total family wealth than younger individuals. As was mentioned in Chapter 3, these correlations may not be of concern. First, couples (assuming there are not complete returns to scale in families) will require a higher level of wealth to achieve the same level of consumption as single people in retirement. Second, older families have had longer to accrue assets – in other words, when the younger individuals are the same age as the older individuals currently are, they may have higher levels of wealth as well. Whether this happens or not depends on younger individuals' behaviour over the next few years. However, across all those aged 55–59, total wealth is, at the median, only 8.6 per cent above that among those aged 50–54. Hence, as long as total wealth increases by 1.7 per cent a year in real terms over the next five years, those aged 50–54 will have a higher level of retirement resources than that currently seen among those aged 55–59. The change in younger individuals' asset holdings over the next few years clearly depends on whether or not they are in paid work in future years – this is examined in Chapter 5.

Table 4.2
Mean and median total family wealth by family type and age (£000s)

	Age				Unweighted N
	50–54	**55–59**	**60–64**	*All*	
Single people	255.0	274.5	300.9	270.1	999
	(161.6)	(180.6)	(228.8)	(178.1)	
Of which:					
Single men	288.3	267.0	300.9	284.4	470
	(191.9)	(180.6)	(228.8)	(193.4)	
Single women	229.9	280.9	n/a	253.8	529
	(149.2)	(180.1)	(n/a)	(164.1)	
Couples	564.7	614.5	617.3	593.6	3,688
	(437.9)	(481.8)	(474.0)	(459.9)	
All	*498.7*	*541.6*	*556.0*	*525.6*	*4,687*
	(377.6)	*(407.6)*	*(419.9)*	*(394.6)*	
Of which:					
Men	506.2	538.5	556.0	531.6	2,626
	(390.4)	(400.7)	(419.9)	(401.6)	
Women	491.0	544.8	n/a	517.1	2,061
	(368.4)	(410.9)	(n/a)	(383.0)	

Notes: Medians are shown in parentheses. One observation per individual aged between 50 and the SPA.

Amongst single people, there is no systematic difference between the wealth held by men and that held by women. In the 50–54 age group, single men are wealthier on average than single women. However, in the 55–59 age group, single women are slightly wealthier than single men. This will be in part because women aged 55–59 are closer to their SPA and can have accrued full entitlement to the basic state pension at this age, whereas men cannot have done so. Therefore, women's pension wealth will be higher, on average, than men's in this age group, as was seen in Table 3.2. Across all men and women, there is also no systematic difference between family wealth for men and family wealth for women. This is what we would expect since single men and single women have similar levels of wealth and (as wealth is defined at the family level) each individual in a couple is allocated the same wealth.

There are other dimensions in which we would expect wealth to vary. One of these is current employment status. Those who are currently in paid work will be more likely to accrue additional wealth before retiring than those who are currently not in paid work. This is particularly true because only a small number of individuals aged between 50 and the SPA who are out of work actually return to work. Therefore, whilst those who are in work may accrue more wealth before retiring, those who are currently out of work will be unlikely to return to work and so their current wealth will more closely reflect the assets that will be available to them to fund their retirement consumption. Table 4.3 shows how wealth varies by employment status and the type of assets held. Individuals are divided into three categories – in paid work, retired and inactive. The distinction between the last two categories is that the members of the 'retired' group are not in paid work but define themselves as retired, whereas the members of the 'inactive' group are out of the

Table 4.3
Distribution of total family wealth by family-level asset holding and individual
employment status (£000s)

	Mean	p25	Median	p75	Unweighted N
All aged 50 to SPA	525.6	225.0	394.6	669.5	4,687
Of which:					
In paid work	544.1	261.2	418.4	681.0	3,191
Retired	751.5	356.1	608.2	885.9	512
Inactive	349.0	99.9	217.1	432.4	984
Those with a house and a private pension	631.4	320.2	490.4	746.8	3,561
Of which:					
In paid work	610.1	317.5	484.2	732.5	2,622
Retired	841.9	455.7	671.2	959.1	438
Inactive	567.6	283.1	413.9	631.6	501
Those with a house or a private pension (not both)	249.8	120.1	189.4	296.9	766
Of which:					
In paid work	277.0	133.3	214.0	320.2	460
Retired	305.3	135.2	211.8	313.5	54
Inactive	186.6	101.6	147.1	213.9	252
Those with neither a house nor a private pension	83.0	51.4	73.3	102.0	360
Of which:					
In paid work	97.7	58.0	74.3	111.7	109
Retired	(92.8)	(75.0)	(84.6)	(108.1)	20
Inactive	75.2	49.3	70.5	99.0	231

Notes: One observation per individual aged between 50 and the SPA, with current employment status
defined at the individual rather than the family level. Those who are in paid work and report being retired are
counted as being in paid work. Where the sample size is small, figures are given in parentheses.

labour market but do not define themselves as retired. Here, we make this distinction at the individual level – so, for example, some 'retired' individuals will have a partner who is in paid work.

The distinction between those who are out of work and consider themselves to be retired and those who are out of work but do not regard themselves as retired is clearly important. Virtually all of those who define themselves as retired (85.5 per cent) have both a house and a private pension. In contrast, only 50.9 per cent of those who are out of work but not retired have both a house and a private pension. This suggests that there is a distinct difference between individuals who define themselves as retired (generally those who are relatively wealthy) and those who are out of the labour market but do not define themselves as retired (generally those who are relatively poor), even though there is only a low chance that any of these individuals will return to work.

Table 4.3 shows that those in the lowest-wealth families are, on average, those who have neither a house nor a private pension. At the median, this group have just £73,000 of total wealth and there is little variation in median wealth by employment status for this group. This level of wealth is far below median wealth across all families, which is £395,000. The wealthiest group is those who have both a house and a private pension and define themselves as retired. This group has median family wealth of £671,000.

It is also clear from Table 4.3 that, on average, amongst those with either a private pension or a house or both, those who define themselves as retired have much higher levels of wealth than those who are either in paid work or out of work but do not consider themselves retired. This suggests that there are three distinct groups of people. First, there are those who are currently in work. These individuals are likely to accrue additional wealth before reaching retirement and currently have slightly lower levels of wealth on average than those who consider themselves to be retired. Second, there are those who are out of work but do not consider themselves to be retired. These individuals are the poorest on average and (we know from evidence of labour market re-entry amongst older people) are fairly unlikely to return to work (and thus unlikely to accrue additional wealth) before reaching the SPA. Indeed, as shown in Section 5.1.2, individuals in lower-wealth families expect lower chances of being in work at older ages than wealthier individuals. This group should perhaps cause greatest concern, since they represent a significant number of individuals in currently low-wealth families who are also unlikely to accrue further wealth before reaching retirement. Finally, there are those who are out of the labour market and define themselves as retired. These individuals are, on average, in the wealthiest families; almost none of this group has neither a private pension nor a house.

We would expect those with high lifetime incomes to have high levels of wealth, since they will have been able to accumulate more wealth in each year throughout their lives. The wealthiest group from Table 4.3 – those who are retired but have both a private pension and a house – are probably high-lifetime-income families. Though they are currently out of work, they probably had high earnings during the rest of their working lives and so have large stocks of wealth that they will use to smooth their consumption through retirement. Therefore, we would expect to see a correlation between lifetime income and wealth. Since we do not have a measure of lifetime income, Figure 4.4 shows the correlation between wealth and current income (as a proxy for lifetime income). Current income is strongly correlated with total wealth – at the median, families in the highest income decile have twice as much wealth as families in the 7th decile, who in turn have twice as much wealth at the median as families in the 2nd decile.[2]

The only part of the income distribution where a positive correlation between income and wealth is not so clear is at the very bottom. The reason for this is at least partly that the bottom decile contains a significant number of self-employed people who made losses in the last year. Therefore their current income appears very low,

---

[2] Single individuals (with no other dependants) in the wealthiest decile have median income of about £34,500 a year. Single individuals (with no other dependants) in the 7th decile have median income of about £15,900 a year. Single individuals (with no other dependants) in the 2nd decile have median income of about £5,700 a year.

Figure 4.4
Distribution of total family wealth by decile of current income

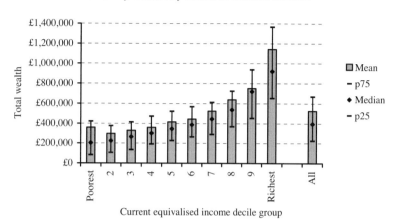

Notes: Sample size = 4,687. One observation per individual aged between 50 and the SPA.

although they may have reasonably valuable business assets and in fact be in relatively high-lifetime-income families.

One very important characteristic of individuals when considering the adequacy of their retirement resources is how long they expect to live. Other things equal, an individual with a given life expectancy will be able to spend twice as much a year as an individual with the same wealth who expects to live twice as long. But other things may not be equal – in particular, poor health may also lead to higher health costs and therefore higher consumption needs in each year of retirement. Section 5.1.3 examines in detail the correlation between wealth and self-reported chances of survival to age 75, but one initial indicator of life expectancy, which is examined in this section, is current health. There is a well-documented correlation between health status and wealth holdings – healthier individuals are generally wealthier.[3] Figures 4.5 and 4.6, which show the cumulative distribution of total family wealth by two different measures of health, show that we find the same result from the ELSA data.

Figure 4.5 shows the cumulative distribution of total family wealth by a very specific measure of health status – whether or not the individual (or, if relevant, their partner) reports having a long-standing illness that limits their daily activity. This shows that healthier individuals have more wealth than less healthy individuals. Whilst 68 per cent of individuals in poor health have wealth of less than £500,000, only 55 per cent of individuals without a limiting health condition have wealth below this level. Similarly, about 64 per cent of healthy individuals have wealth greater than median wealth for unhealthy individuals.

---

[3] Smith, 1999.

However, defining health on the basis of having a limiting long-standing illness is very specific and may not capture certain illnesses that could also result in shortened life expectancy or be associated with lower earnings – for example, mental health conditions. Therefore Figure 4.6 shows the result when we define health on the basis of self-reported health status. All ELSA respondents are asked to

Figure 4.5
Distribution of total family wealth by health status (limiting health condition)

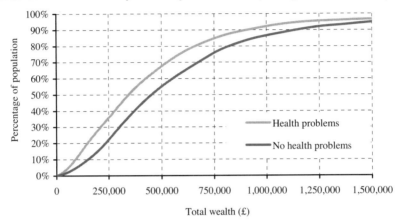

Notes: Sample size = 4,687. One observation per individual aged between 50 and the SPA. A health problem is a long-standing health problem that limits an individual's daily activity. The density functions are estimated using an Epanechnikov kernel with a band width of £40,000.

Figure 4.6
Distribution of total family wealth by health status (self-reported)

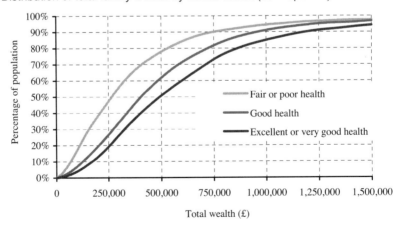

Notes: Sample size = 4,634. One observation per individual aged between 50 and the SPA. The density functions are estimated using an Epanechnikov kernel with a band width of £40,000.

describe their health on a five-point scale from 'excellent' to 'poor'. Figure 4.6 classifies individuals into three groups – those who describe their health as 'excellent' or 'very good', those who describe their health as 'good' and those who describe their health as 'fair' or 'poor'. Using this subjective measure of health, we still find the same pattern between wealth and health as Figure 4.5 demonstrates. Only 51 per cent of individuals who report excellent or very good health have total wealth of less than £500,000, compared with about 62 per cent of individuals who report good health and 78 per cent of individuals who report only fair or poor health.

It is clear there is a strong correlation between wealth and health for ELSA respondents. However, the linkages between wealth and health are fairly complex and it is unclear what the causation is. There are three main reasons that we might observe more low-wealth than high-wealth individuals in poor health. First, the causation could run from health to wealth. Either less healthy individuals anticipate a shorter life and so optimally accumulate a lower stock of wealth to fund their retirement consumption, or less healthy individuals are less able to command high salaries when they are of working age and so are less able to accumulate large stocks of wealth (alternatively, those in low health may have had to spend more on healthcare, which will have reduced the extent to which they can accumulate assets). Second, the causation could run in the opposite direction, from wealth to health. The lifestyles of the wealthy may be healthier than those of the poor and so wealthy individuals are less likely to be in poor health, or wealthy individuals may have better access to healthcare. Finally, there may be unobserved characteristics that are associated with both health and the ability to accumulate wealth – in other words, there is no direct causation from one to the other; there are simply common factors that determine both. For example, family background may influence both health and the ability to accumulate wealth. In practice, all three mechanisms probably contribute to the observed correlation.

We have already examined the distribution of total wealth by various individual characteristics. However, it would also be useful to know which characteristics are most associated with high or low total wealth as this would be useful, for example, in targeting policies at groups with the lowest levels of wealth. Table 4.4 shows the proportions of individuals in each quartile of the wealth distribution who have certain characteristics. It is clear that certain characteristics are particularly associated with low or high wealth. For example, as we have just seen, individuals with health problems are more likely to have low wealth. Of those in the poorest wealth quartile, 46.4 per cent report a limiting health problem, compared with 17.4 per cent of those in the richest wealth quartile and 29.1 per cent among all individuals.

Education and numeracy appear to be important identifiers of wealth for individuals. Among those in the poorest wealth quartile, 58.1 per cent have low education, compared with 13.9 per cent in the richest quartile and 37.2 per cent overall. Similarly, among those in the poorest quartile, only 7.0 per cent are in the highest numeracy category, compared with 30.8 per cent of those in the richest quartile and 17.6 per cent overall.

Women also have a slightly greater chance of being in the poorest quartile. The greatest difference, however, can be seen for separated and widowed women. Taken

Table 4.4

Mean personal characteristics of individuals in each quartile of the distribution of total family wealth (%)

	All	Quartile			
		1 (poorest)	2	3	4 (richest)
Education					
Low	37.2	58.1	46.1	29.6	13.9
Medium	33.6	31.0	33.7	38.8	31.1
High	29.2	10.9	20.2	31.6	55.0
Numeracy					
Level 1 (lowest)	11.0	22.1	10.5	6.7	4.2
Level 2	39.7	48.2	46.0	37.4	26.6
Level 3	31.7	22.6	30.9	35.4	38.4
Level 4 (highest)	17.6	7.0	12.7	20.4	30.8
Female	41.1	43.5	41.1	38.6	41.3
Never married	1.7	3.3	1.6	1.5	0.3
Widowed	2.0	4.1	1.5	1.0	1.3
Separated/Divorced	6.1	16.0	4.9	2.7	0.7
Currently in couple	31.3	20.1	33.2	33.4	38.9
Male	58.9	56.5	58.9	61.4	58.7
Single	11.2	25.7	9.8	6.1	2.8
Currently in couple	47.7	30.9	49.1	55.3	55.9
Health status					
Health problems	29.1	46.4	27.4	24.8	17.4
No health problems	70.9	53.6	72.6	75.2	82.6
Employment status					
In paid work	69.1	53.0	76.0	75.2	72.2
Retired	10.4	5.4	6.9	11.5	18.2
Inactive, not retired	20.5	41.6	17.1	13.3	9.6
Housing tenure					
Owner-occupier	81.9	42.5	90.7	96.3	99.1
Not owner-occupier	18.1	57.5	9.3	3.7	0.9
Pension status					
Ever in private pension	75.2	49.0	78.0	85.8	88.8
Has a current scheme	50.1	28.8	54.8	59.9	57.3
Of which:[a]					
DB	21.6	4.1	15.7	30.9	36.4
Employer DC (no DB)	10.1	9.6	12.9	10.6	7.2
Non-employer DC only	15.9	11.9	22.7	15.8	13.2
No current scheme	25.1	20.1	23.2	26.0	31.5
Receiving income from some/all past pensions	16.3	7.3	14.1	19.6	24.6
Not receiving income from any past pensions	8.8	12.8	9.1	6.4	6.9
Never had a private pension	24.8	51.0	22.0	14.2	11.2

[a] There are also a small number of people (2.5 per cent of the sample) who do not know the type of pension scheme to which they currently belong.
Notes: Sample size = 4,687. One observation per individual aged between 50 and the SPA.

together, they comprise 20.1 per cent of the poorest wealth quartile and just 2.0 per cent of the richest quartile. In contrast, both men and women in couples are more likely to be in the richest decile. Since total wealth is measured at the family level, unless there are complete returns to scale in households couples will require more wealth than single people to provide them with the same level of retirement consumption. To this extent, we would expect to find more couples than single people amongst the wealthier quartiles.

As was shown at the beginning of this chapter, there is a high positive correlation between ownership of different assets. In other words, individuals with high levels of wealth in one form of asset generally have high levels of wealth in all other forms of asset as well. Therefore, individuals who own certain assets are more likely to be amongst the wealthiest families. For example, individuals who have never been a member of a private pension comprise 51.0 per cent of the poorest quartile but just 11.2 per cent of the richest quartile. A similar correlation can be seen for current ownership of houses and membership of private pensions (both current and ever).

So far, we have looked at the correlates with wealth in isolation. To establish whether each of these characteristics is directly correlated with wealth or simply acting as a proxy for another characteristic, Table 4.5 shows the results of a multivariate analysis of total wealth. The results from three quantile regressions (for the 25th, 50th and 75th percentiles) are shown. This is similar to the multivariate analysis of pension wealth presented in Table 3.7. The variables included are deciles of non-pension income (as in Chapter 3, non-pension income is included because of the high correlation, by definition, between pension income and pension wealth), education, gender, family type, employment status, health and age.

In general, the coefficients are higher in absolute value in these regressions than in the regressions using just pension wealth in Table 3.7. This shows that factors associated with higher pension wealth tend also to be associated with higher levels of the other forms of wealth and so are associated with even greater levels of total wealth. For example, being in the top decile of current (non-pension) income is associated with £163,000 of additional pension wealth but £348,000 of additional total wealth at the median. Similarly, higher levels of education (controlling for income and employment status) are associated with greater increases in total wealth than in pension wealth alone – individuals with higher-education qualifications have £150,000 more total wealth and £103,000 more pension wealth at the median than individuals who only have qualifications at A level or below.

Women have higher levels of wealth than men, all other things being equal. Females in couples are found to have £56,000 more wealth than men in couples. While single men have (at the median) £179,000 less wealth than men in couples, single women have £161,000 less.

Health continues to be significantly negatively associated with wealth level, and age continues to be positively associated with wealth level. However, in contrast to the result found in Table 3.7, the coefficient on not being in paid work in the 25th and 75th percentile regressions is now significant. At the 25th percentile, not being in paid work is associated with £46,000 less total wealth. In contrast, at the 75th percentile, not being in paid work is associated with £87,000 higher total wealth. This could be further evidence of the fact that the 'not in paid work' group amongst

Table 4.5
Multivariate analysis of total wealth

	Total wealth (£000s)					
	Quantile					
	25th percentile		50th percentile		75th percentile	
	Coeff.	S.E.	Coeff.	S.E.	Coeff.	S.E.
Non-pension income decile						
2	−32.62	12.74	−52.63	15.91	−53.40	26.51
3	−52.85	13.50	−65.18	16.83	−54.63	34.02
4	−35.62	15.95	−26.04	17.16	−26.59	31.54
5	−38.54	15.24	−74.48	20.08	−64.30	31.88
6	−20.38	17.15	−49.73	18.80	−70.55	27.86
7	5.54	17.81	−15.25	18.47	−3.58	29.64
8	49.85	19.31	50.54	24.60	66.89	34.70
9	111.17	24.85	143.38	25.43	153.99	32.60
Richest	310.95	25.85	347.62	34.21	541.56	41.53
No formal qualifications	−59.06	7.00	−97.49	8.28	−129.47	14.61
Degree	95.97	11.03	150.38	14.90	196.78	17.48
Single male	−126.30	11.12	−179.28	11.41	−248.64	21.12
Single female	−98.07	11.84	−160.67	11.32	−235.11	18.63
Couple female	49.85	9.01	56.22	9.47	64.38	16.41
Not in paid work	−46.39	13.33	11.60	16.69	87.28	33.67
Health problems	−35.61	6.76	−69.02	7.53	−120.39	12.25
Age − 50	9.47	1.16	11.96	1.47	12.38	1.92
(Not in paid work) × (Age − 50)	2.20	1.81	−0.76	1.98	−1.58	3.88
Constant	236.03	19.00	379.28	22.65	568.80	34.32

Notes: The omitted group is 50-year-old men in couples in the bottom decile of current income, who have A levels, are in paid work and report no health problems. Non-pension income is total family unequivalised income from all sources other than pensions. These regressions regress total family wealth on individual characteristics. Sample size = 4,687. One observation per individual aged between 50 and the SPA. Standard errors are estimated by bootstrapping with 100 repetitions.

those aged between 50 and the SPA consists of two distinctly different types of people. First, there are those who are out of work through limited labour market opportunities (perhaps related to ill health), who are likely to have low levels of wealth. Second, there are those individuals who have chosen to retire early and have sufficient wealth to fund an extended number of years in retirement. Members of this group are likely to have high levels of wealth. The correlation between being in paid work and wealth does not vary significantly by age, however.

The overall picture is that those characteristics that are associated with high levels of pension wealth are also associated with high levels of other forms of wealth and hence the correlation with total wealth is even stronger. So there are some groups who simply have low levels of all forms of wealth, whilst others have high levels of all forms of wealth. Table 4.5 shows that the individuals most likely to have low levels of wealth are low-educated, low-income, single men in their early 50s who report current health problems. The group most likely to have high levels of wealth are highly educated, high-income, older couples who do not report having any health problems.

So accumulation of wealth in non-pension assets has not been a substitute for pension saving for most people. Instead, some families have accumulated high levels of wealth in both pension and non-pension assets whilst others have accumulated very little in either. However, current wealth holdings, which are what has been examined so far, are not the only consideration when evaluating the adequacy of individuals' provision for retirement consumption needs. The adequacy could be affected by other factors as well. For example, if individuals expected to receive a large lump-sum transfer in the future (from an inheritance, say), they may optimally hold low levels of wealth at the moment because they know they will be able to fund at least part of their retirement consumption from this future transfer. Alternatively, if individuals expect to die young, they will expect to have a relatively short retirement and so have fewer years of retirement consumption to fund. In this instance, again, they might optimally choose to have low current wealth holdings. These future changes are the topic of Chapter 5, which examines the extent to which low-wealth individuals have high expectations of future events that will either increase their wealth or reduce their retirement consumption needs.

CHAPTER 5
Expectations of Future Circumstances and Resources

The analysis in Chapter 4 showed that a significant proportion of people have few current economic resources to fund their consumption during retirement – for example, Table 4.1 showed that 20 per cent of families had total wealth (including owner-occupied housing wealth) of less than £190,000. If annuitised at a rate of 5 per cent, this would yield a total gross income of about £9,500 a year (or £183 a week). However, the figures considered so far have only looked at the level of resources that families currently hold. People may have expectations about the future that would rationally lead them to hold lower levels of wealth today. These expectations are the focus of Section 5.1.

People aged between 50 and the state pension age (SPA) may be expecting to inherit a large sum of money (possibly from their parents) that would help provide resources for their consumption during retirement. Alternatively, low-wealth individuals may be intending to compensate by retiring later, thus increasing their resources whilst also reducing the length of retirement that they have to fund. Finally, if low-wealth individuals simply anticipate dying sooner, they may rationally accumulate lower levels of wealth in the belief that they will have relatively few years of retirement to fund.

Because expectations form an important part of individuals' current behaviour, ELSA includes a number of questions designed to measure them (see Chapter 2 for a description of how these questions are asked). Such expectations questions have been shown to yield outcomes that can be compared meaningfully with the true distribution of chances of various events occurring within and across different population groups (see Hurd and McGarry (2002), for example, who analyse US data on longevity expectations) and the collection of such data is now becoming common in studies of older populations. Section 5.1 starts by looking at how expectations of receiving an inheritance, being in paid work at certain ages and longevity (in this case, the chances of living to be 75) vary by decile of total wealth.

Section 5.2 considers individuals' expectations about their future resources, in terms of expected future private pension income,[1] and whether those expectations are realistic given their pension wealth. It is important for the policy debate to know whether individuals feel that their resources are adequate and whether they have a realistic expectation of what their resources will provide. The policy debate has brought up the possibility of compulsory retirement saving. If individuals expect greater income from their resources than they will actually get or if low-wealth individuals do not anticipate problems with financing their future consumption needs, it may be that individuals are under-informed about their saving decisions and so compulsion could help. However, if individuals are aware that their resources will provide a low income and that, as a result, they may struggle to meet

---

[1] ELSA wave 1 asks about expectations about future private pension income only. Wave 2, once available, will provide very detailed information about both private and state pension income.

their future consumption needs, it may instead be the case that individuals were simply unable to save more during their lifetimes, even though they were aware of the consequences. In this case, compulsion may not be the best course of action. For these low-income individuals, compulsion would require them either to suffer even lower levels of consumption during their working lives or to dissave or borrow to offset the effect of compulsory pension saving, which would be unlikely to be optimal from a portfolio perspective and, furthermore, would not have the desired effect on net saving.

Finally, Section 5.3 looks at individuals' own expectations of having insufficient resources in retirement and whether these are related to whether they under- or over-estimate the amount they are likely to receive from their private pensions. The definition of sufficient resources will clearly vary across individuals and may well be related to the standard of living an individual has enjoyed during their working life. However, we still find a negative correlation between wealth and expectations of inadequacy.

5.1 Correlation between future expectations and total wealth

5.1.1 Expectations of inheritance

One rational reason for holding currently low levels of wealth could be that an individual expects to receive a large lump sum in the future. The principal source of such a transfer is likely to be inheritances. So perhaps it is the case that currently low-wealth individuals expect to receive large inheritances in the future.

Figure 5.1
Mean self-reported chance of receiving an inheritance by decile of total wealth

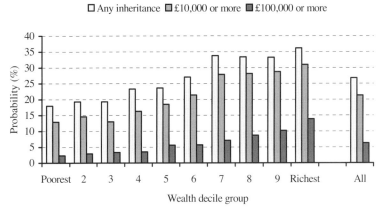

Notes: All figures are weighted. Sample size = 4,510. Details of decile cut points are contained in Table 4.1.

Table 5.1
Distribution of self-reported chances of receiving any inheritance by decile of total wealth

Wealth decile group	Self-reported chance (%)					Unweighted N
	0%	1–39%	40–60%	61–99%	100%	
Poorest	63.6	13.9	10.9	7.7	3.9	436
2	58.4	19.7	8.1	9.2	4.7	444
3	59.9	18.3	8.0	9.2	4.6	437
4	55.0	17.3	11.3	9.9	6.5	443
5	49.1	21.5	13.7	10.6	5.1	448
6	50.7	17.9	10.2	14.6	6.6	456
7	43.6	15.6	12.4	20.9	7.6	455
8	41.1	18.1	14.3	17.2	9.4	453
9	39.4	22.4	10.9	20.0	7.2	465
Richest	41.1	16.7	9.1	24.6	8.5	473
All	*50.0*	*18.2*	*10.9*	*14.5*	*6.4*	*4,510*

Notes: All figures are weighted. Details of decile cut points are contained in Table 4.1.

In fact, Figure 5.1 shows that, far from expecting future inheritances to compensate for their low levels of retirement resources, low-wealth individuals have the lowest average expectations of receiving an inheritance. The wealthiest 10 per cent of individuals on average anticipate that there is a 31 per cent chance they will receive an inheritance of at least £10,000, whereas the poorest 10 per cent of people on average report only a 13 per cent mean chance of receiving such an inheritance. Furthermore, Table 5.1 shows that 63.6 per cent of individuals in the poorest wealth decile expect no chance at all of receiving any inheritance. So it does not appear that low-wealth individuals on average anticipate receiving large lump-sum transfers of this sort in the future.

5.1.2 Expectations of labour market participation

If low-wealth individuals do not anticipate receiving large inheritances in the future, do they instead expect to remain in paid work longer to increase the resources available to them and to decrease the period of retirement that they need to fund? ELSA respondents are asked what the chances are that they will be in paid work at a certain age. That age varies depending on the age and gender of the respondent.

The categories at the left-hand side of Table 5.2 show the ages about which four different gender and age groups are asked. The first column of figures shows the mean expectation of being in work at this age for each group. It shows, for example, that, on average, women aged 50–54 expect a 65.5 per cent chance of being in paid work at age 55. To see how this expectation compares with actual observed employment rates, the next column of the table shows the proportion of individuals at the age asked about (so, for example, in the first row, the proportion of women aged 55) who were employed or self-employed in England in Spring 2004. The actual employment rates shown are the most recent data currently available. It is, of course, possible that employment rates amongst older workers will change by the

Table 5.2
Mean expectation of working at later ages and actual employment rates of
individuals at those ages

	Mean probability	Actual current employment rate
Women aged 50–54: probability of working at age 55	65.5%	68.5%
Men aged 50–59: probability of working at age 60	55.3%	62.8%
Women aged 55–59: probability of working at age 60	35.3%	38.8%
Men aged 60–64: probability of working at age 65	25.3%	25.5%

Notes: The first column of figures is derived from weighted ELSA data (sample size = 4,568). The last column is derived from the English sample of the Spring 2004 wave of the Labour Force Survey (sample size: 884 55-year-old women, 763 60-year-old men, 788 60-year-old women and 609 65-year-old men).

time the ELSA respondents reach the age about which they were asked. However, the trend (over the past 20 years for women and over the last 10 years for men) has been towards higher employment rates for older workers.[2] Therefore, if anything, employment rates amongst older workers in the future are likely to be higher than the 2004 figures shown in Table 5.2.

Comparing the actual outcomes with the expectations shows that (assuming employment rates at each age do not change significantly over the next few years) men aged 60–64 have, at least on average, quite realistic expectations of their chance of being in paid work in the future. On average, they expect a 25.3 per cent chance of being in paid work at age 65; the actual proportion of 65-year-old men in paid work in Spring 2004 was 25.5 per cent. Women in both age groups underestimate their chances of being in paid work by about 3 percentage points – women aged 50–54 report a 65.5 per cent chance of being in paid work, compared with an employment rate of 68.5 per cent for women aged 55 in 2004. The group who underestimate their chances of being in paid work most significantly, however, is men aged between 50 and 59. This group on average predict a 55.3 per cent chance of being in paid work at age 60, whereas in fact 62.8 per cent of men aged 60 were in paid work in 2004. Although this difference is still relatively small, it does suggest that, on average, individuals in these groups may remain in paid work for longer than they currently expect, which for many would boost their retirement provision.

How do expectations of being in work vary across the wealth distribution? Figure 5.2 shows the mean subjective chance of being in work five years before the SPA by decile of total wealth for women aged 50–54 and men aged 50–59. Similar patterns emerge for both groups. Individuals in the lowest wealth decile are the least likely to expect to be in paid work in the future. Men aged 50–59 in the lowest wealth decile report on average only a 37.3 per cent chance of working at age 60, compared with the average across all wealth deciles of 55.3 per cent. Expectations of working then increase towards the middle of the wealth distribution, before falling again towards the top.

---

[2] Source: Banks and Blundell, 2005.

Figure 5.2
Mean self-reported chance of being in work five years before the SPA by decile of total wealth

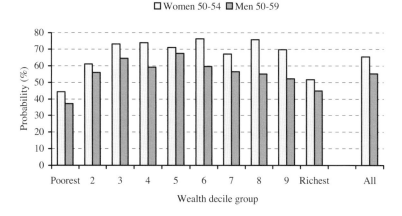

Notes: All figures are weighted. Sample size = 2,756. Women aged 50–54 are asked how likely it is they will be working at age 55. Men aged 50–59 are asked how likely it is they will be working at age 60. Details of decile cut points are contained in Table 4.1.

This pattern at least in part reflects the fact that current employment rates are lower amongst high- and low-wealth groups than amongst middle-wealth groups (Banks and Casanova, 2003). However, the important point in considering individuals' ability to provide themselves with adequate incomes in retirement is whether or not future paid work could boost the currently low levels of wealth held by low-wealth individuals. It appears that, on average, individuals in the middle of the wealth distribution may be planning to boost their retirement resources by retiring later. However, the poorest individuals do not, on average, seem to be planning to do this. This may, however, be rational for those with low levels of resources over their lifetime. First, as we saw in Chapter 4, low wealth is associated with worse health. So less healthy individuals may be less able to work and so it may be rational for less healthy, poorer individuals to expect not to work for longer. Second, poorer individuals face financial incentives that may make working less attractive – alternative income sources (such as the pension credit) will offer relatively high replacement rates for low-wage individuals and the interaction of tapers on benefits such as council tax benefit and housing benefit means that individuals in low-income families face very high marginal tax rates on any earned income (above the earnings disregard in means-tested benefits). Furthermore, for men and women aged between 60 and 64, receipt of the pension credit guarantee is subject to a 100 per cent taper, so there is no incentive to work for individuals who would not earn much more than this level.

Low expectations of working could also be rational for high-wealth individuals. First, wealth effects will cause wealthy individuals to choose to consume more leisure, which could be facilitated by retiring earlier. Second, high-wealth individuals are more likely to experience low or negative private pension wealth accrual[3] if they work until the SPA because they are more likely to be members of defined benefit pension schemes. Negative private pension accrual is most significant in DB pension schemes that have a normal retirement age lower than the SPA. However, it should be noted that, whilst postponing drawing a pension may reduce an individual's pension wealth (because higher annual pension income does not offset the loss of wealth from receiving the pension for fewer years), the annual pension income an individual will receive will still be at least as high if they postpone drawing it, so individuals may want to work in order to increase their annual pension income even if they have negative pension wealth accrual.

Figure 5.3 shows the expectations of working at the SPA for older individuals – women aged 55–59 and men aged 60–64. Banks and Casanova (2003) have shown that only a small proportion of the current generation aged above the SPA are in paid work. The next generation of pensioners is likely to be distinctly different from the current one, in part because of the different state pensions regime that it faces and the higher state pension age for women.[4] However, it is notable from Figure 5.3 that expectations of working past the SPA are also very low amongst those currently within five years of the state pension age. Across nearly all decile groups, the mean reported chance of working at the SPA is under 40 per cent for women aged 55–59 and under 30 per cent for men aged 60–64. The correlation between wealth and work expectations is not as clear for these older groups as for the younger groups shown in Figure 5.2, though. Overall, however, it does not appear that, on average,

Figure 5.3
Mean self-reported chance of being in work at the SPA by decile of total wealth

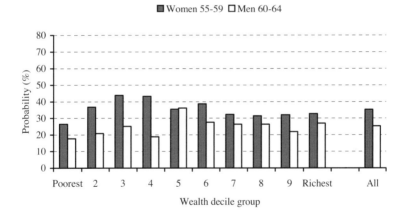

Notes: All figures are weighted. Sample size = 1,812. Women aged 55–59 are asked how likely it is they will be working at age 60. Men aged 60–64 are asked how likely it is they will be working at age 65. Details of decile cut points are contained in Table 4.1.

---

[3] See figure 3.4 in Banks, Emmerson and Tetlow (2005).

[4] The SPA for women will increase by 1 month every 2 months between 2010 and 2020, until the female SPA equalises with the male one.

low-wealth individuals of any age expect to boost their retirement income through working for longer.

5.1.3 Expectations of longevity

If low-wealth individuals do not anticipate working longer, do they anticipate having a shorter retirement because they believe they will die earlier? The correlation between mortality and wealth is well documented: wealthier individuals live longer (see Attanasio and Emmerson (2003), for example, for evidence from the UK). However, the causation could run in either direction, as was discussed in Chapter 4.

ELSA respondents aged between 50 and the SPA are asked how likely it is (on a scale from 0 to 100) that they will live to age 75. Previous work (Banks, Emmerson and Oldfield, 2004) has shown that the responses to this question, on average, understate the likelihood implied by current mortality tables. However, this work has also shown that expectations do vary with factors such as health and gender in the way that we would expect. So, for example, individuals with health problems report a lower chance of survival than healthy individuals.

Using responses to this question, we can look at the extent to which low-wealth individuals expect to die sooner. Whilst we cannot assess the direction of causation, it is informative to know whether individuals with low levels of wealth also expect to die relatively soon and therefore may require less wealth. Figure 5.4 does demonstrate this result – poorer individuals on average report a lower chance of surviving to age 75. The correlation between wealth and self-assessed life

Figure 5.4
Mean self-reported chance of living to age 75 by decile of total wealth and gender

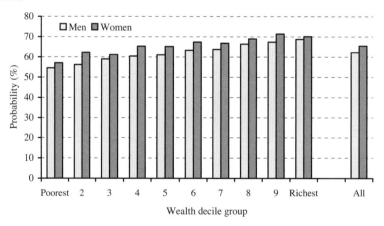

Notes: All figures are weighted. Sample size = 4,528. The mean age of individuals in each decile group does not vary much across the deciles of total wealth, so differences in life expectancy are not simply driven by wealthier individuals being closer to age 75 than poorer individuals. Details of decile cut points are contained in Table 4.1.

expectancy is clearer for men than for women in Figure 5.4, although even for women, wealthier individuals generally report a higher chance of living to age 75. This matches the evidence that suggests that the relationship between current wealth and subsequent mortality is stronger for men than for women (Attanasio and Emmerson, 2003).

Men in the poorest 10 per cent of the population report on average only a 54.5 per cent chance of surviving to 75, whilst women in the poorest 10 per cent report a 57.1 per cent chance. These numbers compare with 68.8 per cent and 70.1 per cent for men and women respectively in the richest decile. So Figure 5.4 shows that, on average, wealthier individuals expect to live longer than poorer individuals – the mean reported chance of living to age 75 is about 14 percentage points higher for men and 13 percentage points higher for women in the richest decile than in the poorest decile.

When considering how adequate individuals' resources are to fund their desired retirement consumption, it is also informative to look at the distribution of responses within each decile – in particular, to look at how many people report very low chances of surviving to age 75 (i.e. whose expected period in retirement is relatively short) and how many people report very high chances of surviving to age 75 (i.e. whose expected period in retirement is relatively long). Figures 5.5 and 5.6 show the proportion of respondents in each wealth decile who report a chance of living to age 75 in certain bands, for women and men respectively. Specifically, they compare across deciles the proportion who think it is very likely they will live to be 75 (61–100 per cent reported chance) and the proportion who think it is very unlikely they will live to age 75 (0–39 per cent reported chance). Figure 5.5 shows that only 41.9 per cent of women in the poorest wealth decile report a chance of survival to age 75 between 61 and 100 per cent, compared with 68.8 per cent of

Figure 5.5
Proportion self-reporting high (61–100%) and low (0–39%) chances of living to 75 by decile of total wealth (women aged 50–SPA)

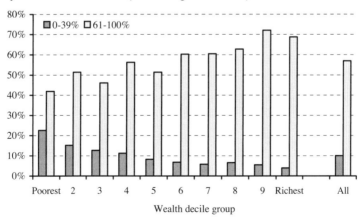

Notes: Sample size = 2,000. Details of decile cut points are contained in Table 4.1.

Figure 5.6
Proportion self-reporting high (61–100%) and low (0–39%) chances of living to 75 by decile of total wealth (men aged 50–SPA)

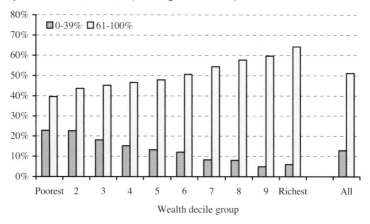

Notes: Sample size = 2,528. Details of decile cut points are contained in Table 4.1.

women in the richest wealth decile. Similarly, Figure 5.6 shows that only 39.6 per cent of men in the poorest wealth decile report a chance of survival in this range, compared with 64.2 per cent of men in the richest decile. The reverse pattern can be seen for individuals reporting being almost certain they will not survive to age 75 (0–39 per cent reported chance).

So there is some correlation between wealth and self-assessed life expectancy. Less wealthy individuals expect to die sooner on average. The possible reasons for the link between health and wealth were discussed in Section 4.4. Here, again, we cannot ascertain in which direction the causality runs, but individuals with lower life expectancies will probably have fewer years in retirement and hence lower total consumption needs.

Having a lower life expectancy reduces the amount of wealth required to fund a given level of consumption each year during retirement from a given age because the individual expects to die relatively soon. This is only true, though, if wealth is held in unannuitised forms and so individuals can choose to consume as much of their wealth each year as they want. However, if wealth is annuitised, individuals will receive a given amount each year for the remainder of their life. Since, for most individually purchased annuities, rates are based on average (gender- and age-specific) life expectancies of annuitants,[5] low-life-expectancy individuals are relatively disadvantaged in the annuity market[6] and cannot choose to receive more

---

[5] Due to adverse selection in the annuity market, even the average annuitant has longer life expectancy than the average person of their age and gender.
[6] Compulsory annuitisation of DC pension funds in the UK partly, though not completely, mitigates this problem (Poterba and Finkelstein, 2002).

income over a shorter period.[7] Instead (for a given size of fund used to purchase an annuity), they receive the same income each year until death as would a higher-life-expectancy individual.[8]

Consequently, lower-than-average-life-expectancy individuals have an incentive to hold wealth in unannuitised forms, whereas higher-than-average-life-expectancy individuals have an incentive to annuitise their wealth, as they are relatively advantaged in the annuities market. This is, of course, only true if individuals anticipated their current health status at the time they were making the decision about the form in which to accumulate their wealth.

Pension wealth is generally annuitised whereas non-pension wealth is generally unannuitised.[9] Table 5.3 shows the proportion of wealth held in pensions (annuitised wealth) for individuals in each wealth decile, split by whether they have above- or below-average expectations of living to be 75. Below-average life expectancy is

Table 5.3
Proportion of total wealth held in pension assets by decile of total wealth and self-reported chance of living to 75

Wealth decile group	Percentage of individuals in this group			Percentage of wealth held in pensions		
	Below-average life expectancy	Above-average life expectancy	*All*	Below-average life expectancy	Above-average life expectancy	*All*
Poorest	59.2	40.8	*100.0*	84.5	80.2	*82.7*
2	54.6	45.4	*100.0*	72.5	72.9	*72.7*
3	55.0	45.0	*100.0*	63.1	60.1	*61.8*
4	49.6	50.4	*100.0*	61.1	56.8	*58.9*
5	51.2	48.8	*100.0*	61.0	57.6	*59.4*
6	46.6	53.5	*100.0*	60.4	60.4	*60.4*
7	43.5	56.5	*100.0*	58.9	58.5	*58.7*
8	41.8	58.2	*100.0*	57.0	59.8	*58.7*
9	36.9	63.1	*100.0*	59.2	57.9	*58.4*
Richest	36.0	64.0	*100.0*	46.7	49.5	*48.5*
All	*46.7*	*53.3*	*100.0*	*62.5*	*59.7*	*61.0*

Notes: All figures are weighted. Sample size = 4,238. Individuals with negative non-pension wealth are excluded since more than 100 per cent of their net wealth is pension wealth. Below-average (respectively above-average) life expectancy is defined as self-reporting a chance of living to 75 that is below (above) the median reported by individuals across all wealth deciles. Details of decile cut points are contained in Table 4.1.

[7] Low-life-expectancy individuals could, to a limited extent, choose to receive more of their annuitised wealth earlier in their retirement by purchasing a nominal annuity, though this obviously does not apply to state pension wealth, which is a particularly large component of total wealth for the poorest individuals.

[8] Low-life-expectancy individuals may, however, be less disadvantaged in DB schemes if they work in an industry in which most employees have lower-than-average life expectancy (such as coal mining), since the generosity of DB schemes in such industries may implicitly reflect the lower-than-average life expectancies of scheme members. See Banks, Blundell and Emmerson (2005).

[9] The one caveat to this distinction is that individuals can, in general, take part (often up to 25 per cent) of their private pension wealth as a lump sum. So approximately a quarter of private pension income is, in fact, unannuitised as well (unless the individual chooses to buy an annuity voluntarily). Furthermore, income draw-down options allow individuals to reduce the level of wealth held in DC pension schemes and so reduce the amount that would have to be annuitised. State pension wealth is entirely annuitised, except for the possibility of delaying receipt in exchange for a lump-sum payment or higher weekly state pension income (the option to receive a lump sum became available in April 2005).

defined as self-reporting a chance of living to 75 that is below the median reported by individuals across all wealth deciles. Ideally, we would look at individuals' survival expectations at the time they were accumulating wealth, since it is possible that individuals accumulated wealth in annuitised assets because they believed they had above-average life expectancy but (due to realisation of subsequent shocks) now believe they have below-average life expectancy. Since we do not have such a measure, we divide people according to their current survival expectations.

First, it is clear that in the lowest three wealth deciles, the majority of individuals have below-average expectations of living to 75. This situation is reversed in the top five wealth deciles, with the 4th and 5th deciles reporting about a 50/50 split. This is the same relationship between current total wealth and expected longevity that was reported in Figure 5.4. Second, the proportion of wealth held in pensions declines as wealth increases. The poorest 10 per cent of individuals hold an average of 82.7 per cent of their assets in pensions, compared with an average of just 48.5 per cent for the wealthiest 10 per cent of individuals. It is not surprising that low-wealth individuals hold virtually all their wealth in pensions whereas wealthy individuals have large amounts of non-pension assets, since a flat-rate state pension system could crowd out all private saving of the poor but leave the rich wanting and able to do lots of private saving. Furthermore, holding wealth in state pensions is sensible for poorer individuals, since it insulates them against risks from changing life expectancy and future asset price shocks.

Low-life-expectancy individuals in the poorest wealth deciles will be less able to reallocate their wealth to the early years of their retirement than wealthier individuals. Since most of the wealth of the poorest individuals is annuitised, they will be forced to receive the same income each year in retirement. A shorter life expectancy will simply mean they receive the income for fewer years. In contrast, low-life-expectancy wealthier individuals, who on average have less of their wealth annuitised, will be able to choose to consume more of their unannuitised wealth in the early years of their retirement because they believe they will not live for very long. So low life expectancy will do little to ease any potential inadequacy in wealth holdings for low-wealth individuals because they will be unable to reallocate their consumption to the early years of their retirement.

5.2 Expectations of retirement income

The previous section has shown not only that there are some people with very low levels of resources to fund their retirement consumption but that these individuals also do not anticipate a high probability of certain future events occurring that would either reduce the demands on their resources or provide them with additional resources. Whether or not these (and other) individuals have realistic expectations about their retirement income is important for the policy debate. If individuals seem under-informed about how much income the resources that they have will generate, one policy response would be to increase the amount or improve the quality of information that individuals receive. In terms of state pensions in particular, the government is already attempting to do this by sending all individuals a state pension forecast. This forecast tells people how much income they can expect to receive from the state pension under a set of assumptions, including that current policy does not change. There are also plans to increase provision of combined pension forecasts that will provide a forecast of both state and private pension income.[10] An alternative policy response would be to force people to save more by introducing compulsory retirement saving (over and above that already implicitly present in state pensions).

If, however, people have very realistic expectations about their future income but yet still have inadequate resources, improving information would be unlikely to encourage them to save more. It is more likely that these people have simply been unable to save more throughout their lifetimes, and so compelling individuals to save more may not be an appropriate course of action.

The first wave of ELSA asks respondents to report the amount of income that they expect from each of their private pensions (which they are not yet receiving).[11] Whilst this is just one component of future retirement resources (and we showed in Chapter 3 that for some groups, it is an important source), there might be a strong correlation between the accuracy of expectations of income from private pensions and the value of other retirement resources. In this section, we first describe the distribution of these expectations and then assess how realistic they are.

5.2.1 The distribution of expected pension income

Table 5.4 shows the distribution of expected annual family-level private pension income (not including any pensions already being received) by decile of total family wealth. Amongst the whole population, mean expected private pension income is

Table 5.4
Distribution of expected annual family private pension income by decile of total wealth (all individuals aged 50–SPA)

Wealth decile group	Mean	p25	Median	p75	Unweighted N
Poorest	£901	£0	£0	£0	438
2	£2,898	£0	£0	£2,515	400
3	£7,298	£0	£2,000	£8,750	368
4	£7,802	£0	£2,500	£9,302	386
5	£6,799	£0	£2,931	£10,375	385
6	£7,866	£0	£2,966	£11,500	388
7	£9,328	£0	£5,000	£12,250	367
8	£11,618	£0	£5,925	£18,750	393
9	£11,278	£0	£5,000	£18,250	418
Richest	£17,698	£750	£10,000	£27,360	421
All	*£8,282*	*£0*	*£2,250*	*£10,750*	*3,964*

Notes: All figures are weighted. Individuals belonging to families where a member does not know how much pension income they are expecting are excluded. Details of decile cut points are contained in Table 4.1.

---

[10] See Department for Work and Pensions (2002).

[11] Wave 2 of ELSA will also ask individuals more detailed questions about how much they expect to receive from both state pensions and total private pensions.

around £8,250 per year while median expected private pension income is only £2,250. This is to be expected, given the skewed nature of the private pension wealth distribution. Expected pension income increases almost monotonically with total wealth.

The amount of pension income that individuals expect, whether that expectation is realistic or not, could be very important for predicting or modelling their behaviour – for example, do people who are expecting higher pension income retire later? However, how realistic those expectations are is perhaps more important for the purposes of policy. While individuals might behave in an optimal way given their expectations, those with unrealistic expectations might have behaved differently if provided with more or better information that made their expectations more realistic. In the next section, we analyse the extent to which individuals over- or under-estimate their future private pension income.

5.2.2 Errors in expectations of private pension income

In order to understand whether or not individuals' expected private pension incomes are realistic, we can compare them with the levels of income that would be generated from their calculated current private pension wealth.[12] There are two limitations in doing this. The first is that the methodology used to calculate pension wealth is complex and depends on a number of assumptions.[13] Furthermore, where individuals are unable to provide information about the characteristics of their pension, imputations have to be made. Inevitably, in these cases, the calculation of private pension wealth (and therefore private pension income) is likely to be less precise. We attempt to take account of this in some of the analysis that follows. The second limitation in making the comparison is that we have relatively little information about some private pensions – notably past private pensions – on which to base the calculation of private pension wealth. Where we have less information about a private pension, it could be argued that our estimate of income from that private pension is no more likely to be correct than the estimate that the individual gives. For this reason, we carry out two comparisons in Table 5.5. In the first, we compare expected income from all private pensions that an individual has (including those that we have less information about) and the income that we predict they will receive based on calculated private pension wealth (hereafter referred to as 'predicted private pension income'). In the second comparison, we restrict our attention to current private pensions because we have a great deal of information about current schemes and so the calculation of pension wealth from these schemes should be more precise. However, the vast majority of individuals with current private pensions are currently in work. There might be less concern about the adequacy of retirement savings for this group and they may also be more

---

[12] Where individuals with DB pension schemes report that they will receive a lump sum from their pension when they retire, we do not include this in our prediction of future pension income. Therefore these individuals' expectations of pension income could exceed our predictions, if individuals do include the annuitised value of these lump sums in their expectations of future pension income. This does not apply to individuals with DC pensions, since our predictions of their pension income are based on annuitisation of their entire fund.

[13] For a summary, see Chapter 2, or see Banks, Emmerson and Tetlow (2005) for more details on the methodology used to calculate private pension wealth.

likely to have a better idea about their expected income in retirement than those with past private pensions that they are yet to draw.

For each private pension, the question that individuals are asked in ELSA is 'How much do you expect to get from this pension when you retire?', and so one issue that will be important is when an individual expects to retire. We use two measures of private pension wealth – private pension wealth if the individual retired at the time of the survey (2002) and private pension wealth if the individual retired at the state pension age. In the latter measure, those who are currently contributing to a private pension are assumed to continue to contribute at the same rate between 2002 and the year in which they reach the SPA. We take three approaches. The first is to compare expected private pension income with predicted private pension income if the individual retired at the time of the survey (referred to as 'retire in 2002' in Table 5.5). The second approach is to use predicted private pension income if they retired at the time of the survey for those individuals who are not working and to use predicted private pension income if they retired at the SPA for those who are working (referred to as 'baseline'). The third approach is to use predicted private pension income if the individual retired at the state pension age for all individuals (referred to as 'retire at SPA'). Although the 'retire at SPA' can be thought of as an upper bound on predicted private pension income, this is only true if the assumption that we made on future private pension contributions (that the contribution rate remains constant until the SPA) is correct. If individuals plan to increase their contribution rate, calculated private pension wealth at the SPA (and therefore predicted private pension income at the SPA) will be underestimated. The baseline measure, which is our preferred method, lies somewhere between the 'retire in 2002' and the 'retire at SPA' measures.[14]

The first three columns of Table 5.5 show mean predicted gross private pension income using the three methods described above. The fourth column shows the mean self-reported expected private pension income.[15] The differences between each of the first three columns and the fourth column therefore reveal the extent to which respondents' expectations differ from our predictions.[16] The upper part of the table shows the predicted and expected private pension income from all private pensions (that are not yet being received) and the lower part shows the values for current private pensions only. In contrast with Table 5.4, the values in Table 5.5 are reported at the individual level. The table contains only individuals who have a private pension from which they are not yet drawing income – this group represents 59 per cent of those aged between 50 and the SPA.

---

[14] Note that the 'retire in 2002' measure does not strictly lie below the 'retire at SPA' measure because for individuals who have past pension schemes that they left before 1988 and in which they have retained rights, the income from those pensions is usually fixed in nominal terms, so income in 2002 is worth more than income if the individual retires at the SPA.

[15] Note that individuals are not asked whether their reported expected income is gross or net of tax.

[16] Where expected private pension income exceeds our prediction, we interpret this as an overestimate by respondents. It is possible, of course, that respondents' expectations are correct and our predicted private pension incomes are underestimated. However, validation of calculated pension wealth in Banks, Emmerson and Tetlow (2005) reveals that pension wealth of those currently approaching the SPA will yield higher income than is currently received by the cohort of individuals who have just passed the SPA. Therefore there is no reason to believe that our prediction of private pension income for those approaching the SPA is, on average, an underestimate.

Table 5.5
Predicted and expected future annual private pension income by decile of
non-pension wealth (individuals with additional expected future private
pension income)

Non-pension-wealth decile group	Mean predicted private pension income (£ p.a.)			Mean expected private pension income (£ p.a.)	Unweighted N
	Retire in 2002	Baseline	Retire at SPA		
All private pensions					
Poorest	3,214	3,710	3,602	4,653	97
2	3,682	4,565	4,546	7,096	171
3	4,508	5,387	5,322	7,174	224
4	4,871	6,336	6,282	8,105	209
5	5,691	7,431	7,431	8,671	220
6	5,573	7,153	7,180	10,518	256
7	7,023	9,533	9,543	12,375	252
8	8,777	11,641	11,655	13,421	231
9	7,247	8,848	8,964	12,393	260
Richest	13,123	16,433	17,393	14,828	264
All	*6,745*	*8,607*	*8,720*	*10,463*	*2,184*
Current private pensions only					
Poorest	4,943	6,059	6,120	7,658	46
2	4,011	5,330	5,378	8,131	125
3	4,387	5,647	5,673	7,688	175
4	5,169	7,000	7,028	8,940	173
5	5,983	8,261	8,276	9,166	181
6	5,760	7,635	7,668	11,396	227
7	7,615	10,519	10,552	13,486	220
8	9,613	13,018	13,072	14,996	196
9	8,399	10,393	10,573	14,404	212
Richest	14,934	19,255	20,528	16,709	211
All	*7,487*	*9,881*	*10,076*	*11,860*	*1,766*

Notes: Individuals who cannot or will not provide an estimate of their future private pension income are
excluded from this analysis. We look at this group separately later. Details of decile cut points are provided in
Table 4.1.

On average, individuals expect to receive £10,463 per year income from their
private pensions. Compared with predicted private pension income assuming
retirement in 2002 (£6,745), this is a mean overestimate of just over £3,700 per
year. This represents a mean percentage error of around 55 per cent. But, of course,
not all individuals will retire immediately. Using the baseline approach, where
individuals who are currently working are assumed to continue to work and
contribute to their current private pensions at the same rate as they are currently,
predicted private pension income is larger, at around £8,600 per year. Even using
this method, individuals still, on average, overestimate the income they are likely to

receive, although to a lesser extent – by around £1,800 (or 22 per cent) per year. Similar results are obtained using the 'retire at SPA' approach, since the majority (85 per cent) of this sample are currently in paid work.

At the mean, all deciles except the richest overestimate the amount of private pension income they will receive, although there is no systematic tendency for poorer deciles to overestimate by more than richer deciles either in levels or in percentage terms.

The lower half of Table 5.5 shows mean expectations errors surrounding current private pensions only. The vast majority (94 per cent) of these individuals are currently in paid work and so predicted private pension income for 'retire at SPA' and for 'baseline' are very similar. Using the 'retire in 2002' method, we find that individuals overestimate by over £4,000 per year on average, but using the baseline method, we find the mean error is smaller (around £2,000 per year). As we discussed above, the calculations of private pension wealth are likely to be more precise for current private pensions than for past private pensions due to the larger amount of information collected about current private pensions. Since the extent to which individuals overestimate their private pension income from current pensions is very similar to the overestimation in private pension income from all private pensions, it is unlikely that the results in the top half of Table 5.5 are purely due to the way in which private pension income from past private pensions is calculated.

Although there is little empirical evidence in this area, Ghilarducci (1992), using data from the US, does show that individuals in DB occupational pensions tend to overvalue their pension rights quite heavily relative to the valuations of either the employer or the scheme actuaries. Part of this may be due to underestimating the extent of early withdrawal penalties. Hence, there are some individuals who we might anticipate should have expectations of private pension income that more closely reflect our predictions. In particular, individuals with relatively straightforward pension arrangements might have smaller expectations errors. If we look solely at individuals who are currently members of one DB pension, who know both when they joined the scheme and what the accrual rate is, and who have never been members of any previous private pension, we find that they do indeed, on average, expect their private pension income to be close to what we predict. Amongst these individuals (who comprise around one-in-five of those with a private pension that they are not yet drawing), average expected pension income is £13,071 a year compared with predicted pension income of between £11,418 and £15,795, depending on whether they retire in 2002 or work to the SPA. In other words, we can find groups of individuals that have expectations in line with our predictions. Individuals who have been members of several pensions during their lives, or those with DC pension arrangements, may have less accurate expectations of their future pension income because their private pension income is more complicated to estimate. Of course, individuals who have only ever had one private pension are also much more likely to have been in this pension for a long time and therefore have had a longer period during which to learn how their pension works.

The results in Table 5.5 suggest that, on average, individuals are overestimating the amount of private pension income that they will receive, and for some individuals this error is large in percentage terms. However, the results are an average of individuals who overestimate their private pension income and those who underestimate their private pension income. Policymakers may be concerned about the direction of the expectations errors. Although the optimal situation for an individual is to know as precisely as they can the amount of income they will receive in retirement, individuals who underestimate will presumably be pleasantly surprised when they reach retirement and may be less of a concern than individuals who overestimate their private pension income.

Table 5.6 shows the percentage of individuals with errors within plus or minus 30 per cent of their predicted private pension income, the percentage overestimating by more than 30 per cent and the percentage underestimating by more than 30 per cent. The numbers show that over 45 per cent of all individuals with future private pensions overestimate the amount of private pension income they will receive by more than 30 per cent.[17] Less than a quarter expect an amount within 30 per cent of what we predict they will receive and nearly a third underestimate by more than 30 per cent. Those in the poorest non-pension-wealth quintile are more likely than those in the richest quintile to overestimate their private pension income by more than 30 per cent. One partial explanation for the size of the group that overestimates is that individuals who have current private pensions to which they are still contributing might be planning to increase their contribution rate (rather than continuing to contribute at their current rate, which is what we assume in the 'retire at SPA' approach). However, the size of the group and the extent of the overestimation make this unlikely to be the full explanation of why individuals overestimate their future private pension income.

These figures reveal that there are substantial numbers of individuals who might benefit from more information or different information about their private pension scheme(s) and, in particular, the income that they are likely to receive from that pension. However, it is not necessarily the case that providing people with this information will directly lead to an increase in the amount that they choose to save in their private pensions. Both those who are overestimating and those who are

Table 5.6

Percentage of individuals who over- or under-estimate future private pension income by non-pension-wealth quintile (individuals with additional expected future private pension income)

Non-pension-wealth quintile group	Percentage reporting errors in the range:			Total	Unweighted N
	−100% to −30% (underestimators)	−30% to +30%	> +30% (overestimators)		
Poorest	25.8	17.9	56.3	*100.0*	268
2	30.7	24.7	44.6	*100.0*	433
3	31.9	21.4	46.6	*100.0*	476
4	27.3	26.7	46.0	*100.0*	483
Richest	31.9	24.2	43.9	*100.0*	524
All	*29.9*	*23.5*	*46.6*	*100.0*	*2,184*

Notes: Individuals who cannot or will not provide an estimate of their future private pension income are also excluded from this analysis. Details of quintile cut points are given in Table 4.1.

---

[17] Note that the results in Table 5.6 are affected little by the inclusion of individuals whose private pension wealth was calculated using imputed data.

underestimating their private pension income could choose to save less as a result of receiving better information.[18]

In order to understand which characteristics are associated with less realistic expectations, we carried out multivariate analysis of the expectations error using a number of characteristics, including age, education, numerical ability, employment status and health. Because we might expect our estimates of private pension wealth to be less precise for respondents for whom imputation was used to calculate private pension income, we carried out the analysis on respondents who were able to provide all the information required to calculate their private pension income. However, because the group of respondents for whom we did carry out imputation are likely to be a non-random sample of individuals, we used a selection model that corrects for any resulting bias in the results. In the same way, we also took account of the fact that some individuals were unable to provide an estimate of their expected private pension income. The full results of this analysis are reported in Table A5.1 of the appendix to this chapter. We ask whether there are any characteristics that are associated with a large absolute expectations error. The results show that after controlling for other characteristics, relative to men in couples, single men and women in couples have a larger absolute difference between our prediction and their expectation on average, and working individuals have a smaller absolute difference on average than individuals not in paid work. Relative to those in the poorest non-pension-wealth decile, the 5th and 10th decile groups have a smaller absolute expectations error on average.

The analysis of expectations error so far has been based on individuals who are able to provide an estimate of the private pension income that they expect when they retire. However, 20 per cent of individuals who have a future private pension on which they will be able to draw are unable to give any estimate at all. This group of individuals would be a prime target group for the policymaker in terms of increasing their knowledge and understanding about their private pensions. Multivariate analysis of this group (full results are reported in Table A5.2 of the appendix) shows that individuals with a very low level of numeracy are less likely than their more numerate counterparts to be able to provide an estimate of their future private pension income (i.e. the coefficient reported in Table A5.2 is positive) and those in the richest two non-pension-wealth deciles are more likely to be able to provide an estimate of their future private pension income.

Taken together, this evidence suggests that there may be some systematic mis-estimation of the incomes that people's private pensions will provide, and that this is more common in some groups than in others. This is clearly a topic that warrants further research, not least because the government has, since the collection of the 2002 ELSA data, issued individuals with state pension statements and is encouraging them to get combined pension statements that include any private pensions they may have. The success or failure of such a policy in closing the information gap is clearly important.

---

[18] Those who were overestimating their likely private pension income might be expected to save more. However, this is not necessarily the case – if they are overestimating likely future annuity rates, then better information could lead to them choosing to save less than they are currently saving. This is because the 'price' of retirement consumption is higher than they currently believe. Similarly, those who are currently underestimating likely future annuity rates could choose to save more because the 'price' of retirement consumption is lower than they currently believe.

Further research is also needed because the comparisons we have been able to carry out here have been somewhat unsophisticated, relying on our estimate of future pension income and an individual's single answer to a simple and relatively crude single interview question. Subsequent waves of ELSA data measure pension expectations more scientifically and in more detail, and the availability of additional waves will also make the measures of pension wealth more accurate. For both these reasons, we might expect future research to shed more light on the issue. With this in mind, the analysis of adequacy presented in Chapter 6 looks at the level of pension income that individuals are likely actually to have in the future, regardless of whether their expectation of this level is accurate or not.

5.3   Self-reported chance of insufficient resources

Given the evidence presented in the previous section suggesting that many individuals might be overestimating the income they will receive from their private pensions and that (particularly poorer) people have only low expectations of events that may increase their wealth between now and retirement, one further interesting question is whether or not individuals expect to struggle financially in the future. In other words, do they think that their current retirement provision (and plans for improving it in the future) is adequate?

Respondents in ELSA are asked 'What are the chances that at some point in the future you will not have enough financial resources to meet your needs?'. The definition of adequacy is clearly subjective – and indeed might well depend on the level of resources that an individual has enjoyed during their life so far – but the answers do give us some indication of whether individuals with low wealth chose to save little because they believe that will be all they need or whether they have simply been unable to save as much as they now believe they will need.

Figure 5.7 shows that the mean expected chance of having inadequate resources in the future declines with increasing total wealth. Individuals in the bottom decile expect, on average, that there is at least a 50 per cent chance that their financial resources will be insufficient to meet their future needs. The richest decile, on the other hand, expect, on average, only slightly over a 20 per cent chance of being unable to meet their needs in the future. So, low-wealth individuals do anticipate a greater chance of being unable to meet their future needs. However, all groups, even the wealthiest, believe there is a non-negligible chance of this happening, though (as already mentioned) what these needs are may vary across the decile groups. Also shown on Figure 5.7 are the 25th percentile, median and 75th percentile of the expected chance of having inadequate resources for each decile of the wealth distribution. These show that in all but the richest 10 per cent of the population, there is considerable variation in responses to the ELSA question within each decile. For example, even within the 5th, 6th, 7th, 8th and 9th deciles of the wealth distribution, a quarter report at least a 50/50 chance of having inadequate resources at some point, and a further quarter report no more than a one-in-ten chance of having inadequate resources.

Figure 5.7
Mean expected chance of having insufficient resources at some future time
by decile of total wealth

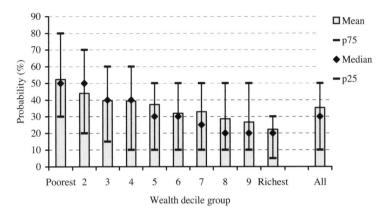

Notes: All figures are weighted. Sample size = 4,510. Details of decile cut points are provided in Table 4.1.

Figure 5.7 shows that poorer families expect a higher chance of having inadequate resources in retirement. However, as this chapter has discussed, the level of wealth that an individual will need to fund their retirement consumption will depend on their expectations of future events. Table 5.7 shows the results of a simple multivariate analysis of the reported chance of having sufficient resources in the future on various individual characteristics, including the self-reported chances of receiving a large inheritance, working in later life and living to the age of 75 (which were discussed in Section 5.1).

The table shows that, conditional on the other characteristics, wealthier individuals still report (at the mean) a lower chance of having insufficient resources in the future. The wealthiest 10 per cent of individuals report a 28 percentage point lower chance than the poorest 10 per cent.

Though it was discussed before that less healthy individuals may have lower retirement consumption needs and therefore may need lower wealth than healthier individuals, Table 5.7 shows that (conditional on the reported chance of living to 75 and on current wealth) individuals with a limiting health problem report a 4.9 percentage point higher chance of having insufficient resources in the future than healthy individuals. This could be because they anticipate having higher healthcare costs than healthy individuals do.

Being in paid work is not significantly associated with expectations of having inadequate resources. However, expectations of working in the future are. Amongst both men of all ages and women aged less than 55, those individuals who report a high chance of working in the future on average report a higher chance of having inadequate resources in the future. On average, men who report a 10 percentage point higher chance of working (at either 60 or 65) also report about a 1 percentage point higher chance of having insufficient resources. For women aged under 55, the differences are slightly lower – on average for women in this age group, a 10 percentage point increase in the chances of working at age 55 is associated with a 0.7 percentage point increase in the chances of having insufficient resources. For women aged 55–60, there is no statistically significant relationship between the chances of working in the future and the chances of expecting insufficient resources. The fact that, for men in particular, there is a strong relationship between the chances of working and the chances of expecting inadequate resources could be an indication that individuals who are concerned about the adequacy of their savings are planning to work for longer in order to compensate for currently lower-than-desired levels of wealth.

Table 5.7

Multivariate analysis of expectation of having insufficient resources in the future (all individuals aged 50–SPA)

	Coefficient	Standard error
Total wealth decile group		
2	−8.49	1.911
3	−13.42	1.987
4	−13.44	2.005
5	−15.08	2.018
6	−20.53	2.043
7	−19.05	2.062
8	−22.98	2.094
9	−24.28	2.104
Richest	−28.40	2.128
High education	−0.08	0.925
Couple	1.54	1.146
Health problem	4.90	0.987
In paid work	−1.68	2.300
(In paid work) × (Age − 50)	0.36	0.286
Age − 50	−0.43	0.297
Expected chance of living to 75	−0.09	0.018
Expected chance of inheriting ≥£100,000	−0.03	0.021
Female 50–54	−0.51	2.232
Female 55–59	2.20	1.686
Male 60–64	0.09	2.374
Expectation of working (male 50–59)	0.10	0.027
Expectation of working (male 60–64)	0.12	0.023
Expectation of working (female 50–54)	0.07	0.019
Expectation of working (female 55–59)	0.04	0.032
Constant	53.48	2.659

Notes: Coefficients were estimated using an ordinary least squares (OLS) regression. Baseline – poorest wealth decile, not employed, low education, no health problems, single man aged 50 and expecting no chance of living to age 75, no chance of working at age 60 and no chance of receiving an inheritance of £100,000 or more. Sample size = 4,436.

The coefficient on expectations of life is the opposite of what we might expect – individuals with higher expectations of living to age 75 report lower chances of having inadequate resources. The association is quantitatively small, however: a 100 percentage point increase in the reported chance of living to 75 (i.e. the difference between someone who is certain they will not and someone who is certain they will) is associated with a 9 percentage point lower reported chance of having insufficient resources. This apparent association could be due to unobserved heterogeneity, such as some individuals being more optimistic and therefore reporting both high chances of living to 75 and low chances of having inadequate resources.

Following the finding in Section 5.2 that, on average, individuals with private pensions overestimate the income they will receive from these pensions, it would be interesting to know whether individuals who have unrealistically high expectations of future pension income in fact have lower expectations of having insufficient resources in the future, and whether the reverse is true for those who underestimate their future pension income. Table 5.8 shows the results of a second multivariate analysis of the reported chance of having insufficient resources. The sample is restricted to those individuals who have a private pension from which they are not yet receiving an income and the regression includes two additional dummy variables. The first of these identifies those individuals who underestimate future pension income by at least 25 per cent. The second identifies those individuals who overestimate by at least 25 per cent. The base group is those individuals who expect pension income within plus or minus 25 per cent of their predicted income.

Table 5.8 shows that, conditional on other characteristics, individuals who significantly underestimate future pension income report nearly a 5 percentage point higher chance of having insufficient resources in the future than individuals who estimate their future pension income approximately correctly. For this group, it is possible that, if they knew how much they were actually likely to receive from their private pensions, they would be less likely to expect to have inadequate resources.

However, Table 5.8 also shows that individuals who overestimate their future pension income also report higher chances (about 3 percentage points higher) of having inadequate resources than individuals who estimate approximately correctly. In other words, this group of people not only expect more income than they are likely to receive but also expect that this income is more likely to be inadequate.[19]

This section has shown that wealthier individuals report lower chances of having insufficient resources than low-wealth individuals. However, even the wealthiest individuals on average report some chance of having insufficient resources at some point in the future. It is possible that individuals' definitions of adequacy vary and are to some extent based on the income they have enjoyed during their working lives, so what a high-lifetime-income individual would regard as insufficient may be very different from what a low-lifetime-income individual would regard as insufficient. It is not possible to tell from the subjective response to the question in ELSA what benchmark individuals are measuring their future provision against. Therefore Chapter 6 looks at individuals' predicted future incomes relative to certain predetermined benchmarks, using both a benchmark defined relative to the

---

[19] It could be that, whilst members of this group overestimate on average, they also expect a larger variance in their expectations of future pension income. Therefore, they also expect higher chances of having inadequate resources.

average economy-wide standard of living (i.e. at the same level for all individuals) and benchmarks defined relative to an individual's standard of living during their working life.

Table 5.8

Multivariate analysis of expectation of having insufficient resources in the future (individuals with private pension)

	Coefficient	Standard error
Total wealth decile group		
2	−10.65	3.224
3	−16.03	3.171
4	−14.17	3.207
5	−17.52	3.210
6	−20.97	3.238
7	−19.72	3.231
8	−23.26	3.281
9	−23.79	3.320
Richest	−27.71	3.319
High education	0.06	1.228
Couple	1.58	1.515
Health problem	5.04	1.342
In paid work	−3.57	3.617
(In paid work) × (Age − 50)	−0.51	0.485
Age − 50	0.46	0.466
Expected chance of living to 75	−0.07	0.024
Expected chance of inheriting ≥£100,000	−0.04	0.025
Female 50–54	−3.45	3.546
Female 55–59	2.07	2.491
Male 60–64	3.57	3.348
Expectation of working (male 50–59)	0.12	0.040
Expectation of working (male 60–64)	0.12	0.032
Expectation of working (female 50–54)	0.07	0.022
Expectation of working (female 55–59)	0.01	0.041
Expects pension income at least 25% below predicted	4.83	1.664
Expects pension income at least 25% above predicted	3.05	1.504
Constant	51.60	4.496

Notes: Coefficients were estimated using an ordinary least squares (OLS) regression. Baseline – poorest wealth decile, not employed, low education, no health problems, single man aged 50 and expecting no chance of living to age 75, no chance of working at age 60, no chance of receiving an inheritance of £100,000 or more and pension income within 25 per cent of predicted level. Sample size = 2,599.

Appendix. Regression results

Table A5.1
Multivariate analysis (selection model[a]) of absolute expectation errors: all individuals who have a future private pension

	Abs[ln(Expected private pension income) − ln(Predicted private pension income)]	
	Coefficient	Standard error
Non-pension-wealth decile group		
2	−0.328	0.205
3	−0.281	0.189
4	−0.279	0.192
5	−0.442	0.196
6	−0.054	0.194
7	−0.272	0.191
8	−0.256	0.189
9	−0.222	0.189
Richest	−0.448	0.189
High education	−0.124	0.089
Single female	0.105	0.137
Single male	0.299	0.125
Female in couple	0.196	0.085
Has limiting long-standing illness	0.103	0.086
In paid work	−0.633	0.199
Age − 50	−0.057	0.043
(Age − 50) squared	0.002	0.003
(Age − 50) × (In paid work)	0.051	0.024
Numeracy level 1 (lowest)	0.302	0.185
Numeracy level 2	0.173	0.190
Numeracy level 3	0.078	0.206
Constant	1.487	0.344

[a] The selection equation is a probit of a variable that takes the value 1 for individuals who had no components of their pension wealth imputed and who know their expected private pension income. The same variables are included as regressors with the addition of dummy variables to identify each interviewer which are excluded from the main stage of the regression.
Notes: Sample size = 2,691. Baseline – poorest wealth decile, low education, man in a couple, aged 50, no health problems, not in paid work, high numeracy level.

Table A5.2
Multivariate analysis (probit model) for those who do not know their
expected private pension income: all individuals who have a future private
pension

	Marginal effect	Standard error
Non-pension-wealth decile group		
2	0.003	0.042
3	−0.054	0.036
4	−0.009	0.040
5	0.009	0.042
6	−0.066	0.034
7	−0.069	0.034
8	−0.037	0.038
9	−0.076	0.034
Richest	−0.080	0.034
High education	−0.012	0.018
Single female	0.025	0.028
Single male	0.001	0.028
Female in couple	0.009	0.019
Has limiting long-standing illness	0.004	0.019
In paid work	0.054	0.044
Age − 50	−0.014	0.010
(Age − 50) squared	0.003	0.007
(Age − 50) × (In paid work)	0.001	0.001
Numeracy level 1 (lowest)	0.121	0.042
Numeracy level 2	0.028	0.023
Numeracy level 3	0.019	0.022

Notes: Sample size = 2,709. Baseline – poorest wealth decile, low education, man in a couple, aged 50, no
health problems, not in paid work, high numeracy level.

CHAPTER 6
Identifying Those at Risk of Having Inadequate Retirement Resources

Chapter 3 showed that a reasonable proportion of the population had relatively low levels of private pension provision, with a quarter of those aged between 50 and the state pension age (SPA) having yet to accumulate any private pension wealth at all. The analysis in Chapter 4 showed that the distribution of non-pension wealth was extremely skewed and was *positively* correlated with both private pension wealth and total pension wealth. Hence, for many individuals, accumulating assets in non-pension forms has not been a substitute for accumulating pension wealth. Indeed, as was shown in Table 4.1, a fifth of those aged between 50 and the SPA had accumulated less than £189,900 in assets (including housing wealth). The general picture of different dimensions of retirement resources tending to reinforce, rather than offset, each other was supported further in Chapter 5, which showed that those with low current total wealth did not have particularly high expectations of remaining in paid work at older ages and, on average, had lower expectations of receiving an inheritance. Many also appeared to have over-optimistic expectations of the level of retirement income that their private pensions were likely to deliver.

This chapter brings together the analysis from the previous three chapters in the context of recent policy debate over whether the UK faces any 'pensions crisis'. In particular, it presents the most comprehensive analysis to date of the extent to which those aged between 50 and the SPA are able to expect to have 'adequate' resources in their retirement. While younger groups might be of greater concern for policymakers (since they are the ones whose environment, in terms of life expectancy, generosity of state pensions, and expected asset returns, might have changed the most), they are also the groups for whom there is the most time in which their behaviour can adjust. In contrast, the savings and pensions of our age group will largely be determined already, so their current circumstances form a good basis on which to predict retirement outcomes.

The analysis in this chapter models the extent to which individuals are likely to accumulate 'adequate' resources for their retirement. We do this by comparing our estimates of individuals' future retirement incomes and simple benchmark levels that have been used in the policy debate. We do not assess the economic optimality of retirement savings relative to the levels that would be predicted by an economic model that takes into account the full array of past incomes and circumstances as well as current circumstances and expectations for the future. Such an analysis (along the lines of Scholz, Seshadri and Khitatrakun (2004)) will be possible as more waves of ELSA data become available, and is a natural topic for future research. In the mean time, the richness of the data available here nevertheless enables us to extend the existing policy analysis that has been available in the UK.

In Section 6.1, we examine the likely size of future retirement resources among those aged between 50 and the SPA. This is more comprehensive than previous studies as it includes both pension and non-pension wealth, as well as incorporating individuals' expectations both of being in paid work and of receiving inheritances at older ages.[1] Section 6.2 compares the expected adequacy of retirement resources among those who are considered to be at risk of having low levels of resources in retirement. This is a key issue since the optimal policy response in the face of individuals having inadequate retirement provision is likely to depend on the extent to which individuals comprehend their circumstances. Finally, in order to suggest the groups on which policymakers should perhaps place the greatest focus, Section 6.3 compares the characteristics of those who are at risk of having inadequate resources under the various definitions and those who are not at risk of having inadequate resources.

6.1 Are many at risk of inadequate resources in retirement?

High-quality microdata (containing information on both individuals' current resources and their expectations of the future) are not, on their own, sufficient to examine the extent to which individuals can reasonably expect to have sufficient resources for their retirement: it is also necessary to take a view on the level of spending power that should be deemed adequate. This section sets out four different benchmarks and provides estimates of the number of individuals who are at risk of having inadequate retirement resources under each benchmark. The first is the level of income provided by the pension credit guarantee (PCG),[2] while the other three all depend on an estimate of the individual's pre-retirement income. For each benchmark, estimates of the numbers at risk are calculated for four different scenarios of future labour market activity among older individuals, for details of which see Section 6.1.1.

6.1.1 A poverty line interpretation of adequacy

One interpretation of adequacy is that a sensible benchmark is the amount needed to ensure that an individual has sufficient resources to avoid poverty throughout their retirement. This could be described as either sufficient to purchase a fixed bundle of goods in retirement or, alternatively, sufficient to be able to enjoy a certain level of consumption relative to the average of those of working age. Either description might suggest a level that does not vary according to an individual's lifetime earnings, although it could vary with other circumstances – for example, the amount needed by those in couples compared with single individuals, or the amount needed by those in relatively good health compared with those in relatively poor health. There is also the question of how the level should be indexed over time. It could be indexed to a price index (such as the Pensioner Price Index, or a more general price

---

[1] For example, a report by Oliver, Wyman & Company (2001), which stated that the UK had an annual £27 billion saving 'gap', calculated what individuals 'should' have saved for their retirement without taking into account their expectations of the future. Given that saving behaviour is intrinsically a forward-looking process, and that £11.3 billion of this 'gap' was from individuals aged 35 or under, this is potentially a considerable omission.

[2] The pension credit guarantee is a reformed version of the minimum income guarantee (MIG), which had itself existed since income support (IS) payments to pensioners were rebranded in April 1999.

index such as the Retail Price Index or the Consumer Price Index) or to the performance of the economy (such as to average earnings or to GDP per head) or in some other way.

One possible benchmark to take is the pension credit guarantee, which in 2005–06 is set at £109.45 per week for a single pensioner and £167.05 for a pensioner couple. This is the level below which (abstracting from the issue of incomplete take-up) the benefit system will not allow incomes to fall. In terms of how this benchmark should be indexed in future, the current government has already committed to increase the pension credit guarantee in line with average earnings in both 2006–07 and 2007–08 (a pledge which was matched at the recent general election by both the Conservative Party and the Liberal Democrat Party[3]) and has previously stated an aspiration to continue to index it in line with average earnings.[4] Hence a threshold set at the level of the PCG and indexed in line with average earnings is one benchmark that we examine. For this, we assume that average earnings grow at 2.0 per cent a year in real terms.[5] In the analysis that follows, we present the percentage of individuals for whom different measures of their potential retirement income would fall below the benchmark of the PCG threshold in the year that they reach the state pension age. Unless incomes in retirement keep pace with this benchmark (which might continue to be indexed in line with average earnings), a greater number of individuals will fall below this benchmark at older ages.

Finding that some people are predicted to have retirement resources below the level of the PCG (or, indeed, any other benchmark) does not necessarily imply that these individuals have behaved suboptimally. As we discussed earlier, 'adequacy' and 'optimality' are very different concepts, and there is a particular characteristic of the pension credit that highlights this. The existence of the 100 per cent taper of the pension credit guarantee makes retirement consumption relatively expensive for individuals who expect to be on a very low income in retirement. In other words, since £1 of private retirement income will reduce the amount of pension credit received by £1 for anyone whose income in retirement is below the level of the full basic state pension, at the margin these people have no incentive to accumulate additional retirement resources.[6]

The percentage of individuals who are predicted to have income below the level of the PCG in the year that they reach the SPA is shown for four different scenarios in Table 6.1.[7] The first column makes the (pessimistic) assumption that everyone aged between 50 and the SPA immediately retired in 2002. If this were so, we estimate that, on reaching the SPA, 21.2 per cent of these individuals would have an income from their pension (state and private) that would fall below the level of the

---

[3] See Emmerson, Tetlow and Wakefield (2005) for more details.

[4] Source: Prime Minister's foreword to the 1998 Green Paper on pensions, Department of Social Security (1998).

[5] Table 1.1 of HM Treasury (2000) estimates that underlying productivity growth over the period from 1990Q4 to 1997H1 was 2.0 per cent a year.

[6] Ignoring income disregards.

[7] This table does not show the percentage of individuals who are likely to be eligible for the pension credit, for two reasons. First, some of those not eligible for the PCG will be eligible for the pension credit savings credit. Second, individuals might choose to hold their wealth in certain forms (such as owner-occupied housing or other durables) that will not count against the means test for the pension credit (either guarantee or savings credit component).

Table 6.1

Percentage of individuals predicted to have income below the PCG when they reach the SPA

	(1) Retire in 2002	(2) Probabilistic selection of working to SPA	(3) Work to SPA if currently working	(4) Work to SPA
Pension wealth only	21.2	17.7	13.3	10.4
Non-housing wealth only	14.8	12.9	10.5	7.9
Total wealth	8.9	8.2	7.5	5.5
Total wealth plus expected inheritances	8.3	7.7	7.1	5.2
Total wealth plus expected inheritances plus pension credit	≈0	≈0	≈0	≈0

Note: Sample size = 4,667.

PCG in that year. However, this scenario ignores the fact that individuals may have other financial wealth that they could draw on. Assuming that individuals annuitise all of their non-owner-occupied-housing wealth at a rate of 5.0 per cent, and that for tax purposes this is allocated optimally between individuals in couples,[8] then the proportion that would have an income below the level of the PCG would fall to 14.8 per cent, i.e. just over one individual in seven.

As was shown in Chapter 4, a considerable proportion of wealth is held in the form of owner-occupied housing. For example, Figure 4.3 showed that on average across the wealth distribution, a quarter of wealth is held in owner-occupied housing. This wealth could be used by individuals to provide retirement resources through the use of equity release products (such as home reversion schemes), by downsizing, or by selling and moving into rented accommodation. The last case seems the most relevant when considering the level of the PCG as a benchmark for adequacy of retirement resources. This is because additional government support is available through housing benefit to assist families in rented accommodation with their housing costs. Assuming that all owner-occupied housing wealth[9] is liquidised and annuitised at a rate of 5.0 per cent a year (in addition to non-housing wealth) reduces the percentage of individuals who are predicted to have retirement resources below the PCG to just 8.9 per cent of individuals aged between 50 and the SPA. This is shown in the third row of Table 6.1.

---

[8] Where relevant, the available income is allocated to the partner with the lowest marginal rate. This is also done for the annuity incomes received from owner-occupied housing and from expected future inheritances.

[9] Throughout this chapter, we assume families' net housing wealth does not change in the future; in other words, families do not pay off any outstanding mortgages before retiring. This will understate the true level of housing wealth available to fund retirement consumption if in fact families are planning to pay off their mortgages before retirement. However, outstanding mortgages are not very large amongst this age group. Even amongst those individuals aged 50–54, only 25 per cent of individuals have an outstanding mortgage of more than £15,000 (equivalent to £750 a year of income if annuitised at 5.0 per cent, or £375 if annuitised at 2.5 per cent). If those individuals with large outstanding mortgages actually pay off their mortgage before reaching retirement (without reducing their non-housing wealth), the assumption we make here essentially means that they would need to annuitise less of their housing wealth to achieve the levels of retirement resources described in this chapter.

Receipt of inheritances might boost retirement resources further. Taking into account the annuity value of individuals' expectations of receiving inheritances[10] reduces the proportion that are predicted to have a level of retirement resources below the PCG benchmark to 8.3 per cent, or slightly over one-in-twelve individuals aged between 50 and the SPA.

The final row of Table 6.1 shows the percentage of individuals who would have a level of retirement resources at the SPA below the PCG if all those entitled to the pension credit take it up.[11] As a result, the percentage at risk falls almost to zero – this is because the only individuals with retirement resources below the PCG benchmark would be those individuals whose total wealth (including expected inheritances) is negative, and therefore the equivalent annuity value of their debts plus a maximum pension credit award would not be sufficient to bring them up to the level of the PCG.

All the calculations described in this section so far, reported in the first column of Table 6.1, make the pessimistic assumption (in terms of retirement replacement rates) that individuals immediately left the labour market in 2002. Table 6.1 also presents the percentages of individuals who are predicted to fall below the benchmark level of the PCG in the more realistic scenarios in which some individuals remained in paid work. These calculations assume that individuals in paid work continue to accrue additional entitlement to state pensions, and any private pension entitlement is assumed to accrue according to the rules of the plan and the size of the individual's current contribution. Other net wealth is assumed to remain unchanged in real terms. Therefore, to the extent to which individuals decide to increase any voluntary pension contributions, save from future income into other forms or receive real returns on their wealth, these calculations will tend to *overstate* the percentage of individuals that would fall below the PCG.

The fourth (right-hand) column of Table 6.1 shows the calculations under the other extreme assumption, that *all* individuals are in the labour market between 2002 and the SPA. Under this scenario, just 5.2 per cent of individuals would have an income below the PCG when we consider the annuity value of all of their own wealth (including expected inheritances). This equates to less than one individual in nineteen aged between 50 and the SPA.

This 'work to SPA' scenario is likely to overestimate the extent to which older individuals participate in the labour market. Therefore the second and the third columns of Table 6.1 are based on intermediate assumptions. The third column assumes that everyone who is currently in paid work remains in paid work until the SPA, while everyone who is not currently in paid work remains out of paid work. The second column is computed by taking each individual's self-reported chance of being in paid work at an older age (which was described in Chapter 5) and using it to calculate the chance of being in paid work at the SPA.[12] We then use this

---

[10] We allocate to individuals the greater of (a) the self-reported probability of receiving at least £100,000 multiplied by the annuity value of £100,000 and (b) the self-reported probability of receiving at least £10,000 multiplied by the annuity value of £10,000.

[11] We model entitlement to both the pension credit guarantee and the pension credit savings credit. For details of how these operate, see Disney and Emmerson (2005).

[12] Women aged between 55 and 59 and men aged between 60 and 64 are all asked about the chances of them being in work after their respective SPA. Men aged between 50 and 59 are asked for the likelihood that they will be in paid work after age 60. We adjust this to obtain the chance of being in paid work at age 65 by multiplying their expectation by the mean reported chance of being in work after age 65 among men aged 60

probability to simulate whether the individual will remain in work. If individuals' expectations are, on average, correct, then this scenario will be based on the correct proportion of individuals in the labour market.

Under this probabilistic scenario, the percentages who are deemed to be at risk from having a retirement income below the PCG are between those that result from assuming everyone retires immediately (column 1) and those that result from assuming everyone remains in their current labour market status until they reach the SPA (column 3). This is because, on average, those out of the labour market report a very low chance of being in work at older ages, while those who are in paid work report a higher, but less than certain, chance of being in work at older ages. Focusing on this probabilistic way of determining whether or not individuals remain in the labour market suggests that 12.9 per cent of individuals aged between 50 and the SPA will have non-housing wealth worth less than the PCG when they reach the SPA. Including both owner-occupied-housing wealth and expected inheritances, this proportion falls to 7.7 per cent, which is equivalent to just over one individual in thirteen of those aged between 50 and the SPA in England.

Choosing the level of the PCG against which to measure 'adequacy' of retirement resources makes sense since this is what has implicitly been deemed the minimum amount of income that a pensioner could survive on (given the existence of other means-tested benefits, such as housing benefit and council tax benefit). However, we might be interested in seeing how many individuals are predicted to have retirement resources worth less than some other level of annual income. Therefore, Figure 6.1 presents the distribution of predicted equivalised family gross income at the SPA. It shows the proportion of those aged between 50 and the SPA who are predicted to have retirement resources worth less than any level of annual income that one might wish to choose. The four curves show the total family income that individuals are predicted to receive depending on which of their resources they choose to use to fund their retirement consumption. For example, if families consume just their non-housing wealth in retirement, 39.5 per cent of individuals are predicted to be in families with equivalised income of less than £10,000 a year in retirement. If, however, we assume that families downsize their homes,[13] receive on average the inheritance they are expecting and claim any pension credit to which they are entitled, we find that just 26.3 per cent of individuals are in families with equivalised income below £10,000 a year.

The point at which the 'total wealth' curve meets the 'total wealth + pension credit' curve is the income level at which entitlement to the pension credit is exhausted. It is at a higher level than is currently required to exhaust entitlement to the pension credit savings credit because the entitlement to pension credit included in Figure 6.1 is based on the level at which pension credit will be in the year each individual reaches the SPA, assuming that the PCG is uprated in line with average earnings growth in the future. Since men who were 50 in 2002 will not reach the SPA until 2017, the level of real income that will be required to exhaust entitlement to the pension credit when these men reach the SPA will be higher than it is now.

---

in our data (which is 41.2 per cent, estimated across 86 individuals). Similarly, women aged between 50 and 54 are asked for the likelihood that they will be in paid work after age 55. We adjust this to obtain the chance of being in paid work at age 60 by multiplying their expectation by the mean reported chance of being in work after age 60 among women aged 55 in our data (which is 45.4 per cent, estimated across 201 individuals).

[13] Figure 6.1 assumes that individuals annuitise half their housing wealth, as discussed in Section 6.1.2, rather than all their housing wealth, which Section 6.1.1 has previously assumed.

Figure 6.1
Distribution of predicted retirement income at the SPA

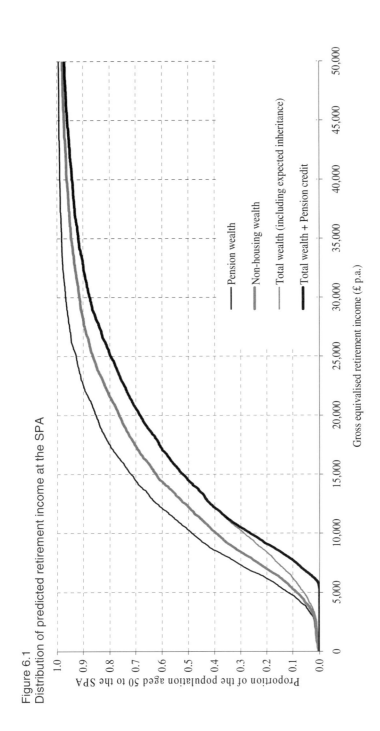

Proportion of the population aged 50 to the SPA

Gross equivalised retirement income (£ p.a.)

———— Pension wealth
———— Non-housing wealth
———— Total wealth (including expected inheritance)
———— Total wealth + Pension credit

6.1.2 An income-related interpretation of adequacy

For some individuals, the PCG will provide a level of income similar to the level that they have had during their working lives.[14] Indeed, those who are in receipt of income support prior to age 60 (from which age both men and women can currently qualify for the PCG) will actually see their income rise if they move onto the pension credit at age 60. For these individuals, it is far from clear that they would prefer greater resources during their retirement as opposed to earlier in their lives. However, for many other individuals, the standard of living implied by the PCG benchmark will be seen as unacceptably low. In this section, we consider an alternative benchmark, with inadequate resources being defined as having retirement resources (net of tax) worth less than a certain percentage of the individual's current net income.

Using a measure net of tax gives a better measure of how an individual's spending power in retirement compares with their current spending power. For those whose current income is at a similar level to the level of income they have typically received during their lives, this measure will show how individuals' resources in retirement compare with those during their working lives. For some individuals, current incomes will reflect lifetime incomes less well. In particular, this might be true of those who have already retired and also of those no longer in their 'main' career who are now in less-intensive and lower-paid work. For these types of individuals, this measure of adequacy will overstate the extent to which their resources in retirement will replace those during their working lives. Nonetheless, for this group, it will still indicate how their income when they reach the SPA will compare with their current income.

A further complication arises over how owner-occupied-housing wealth should be treated. When examining the percentage of individuals whose resources were below the level provided by the PCG in Section 6.1.1, it was appropriate to assume that individuals annuitised the *full* value of their house at 5.0 per cent, since housing benefit would provide assistance with rented housing costs. When assessing how individuals' post-retirement resources will compare with their current resources (as opposed to a poverty benchmark), this assumption does not seem appropriate. However, it is still the case that some housing wealth could be used to provide retirement resources – for example, through a home reversion scheme. Hence, in the remainder of this chapter, when housing wealth is included in retirement resources, we assume that individuals downsize and release *half* of their owner-occupied housing wealth to purchase an annuity at 5.0 per cent. (This is, of course, equivalent to assuming that all housing wealth is annuitised but at the lower rate of 2½ per cent.)

The top part of Table 6.2 shows the percentage of individuals predicted to be at risk of having a 'current income net replacement rate' of less than 67 per cent. (On average, this will translate to a gross replacement rate of slightly more than 50 per cent.[15]) As with Table 6.1, the first column assumes everyone retires immediately in

---

[14] In 2004, the level of the PCG was approximately 20 per cent of average gross full-time earnings in the UK (mean gross weekly full-time pay in the UK was £505 in April 2004 – source: Annual Survey of Hours and Earnings 2004, http://www.statistics.gov.uk/downloads/theme_labour/ASHE_1998_2004/Table3.xls).

[15] Paragraph 3 of annex 4 of Department for Work and Pensions (2002) states that for an individual earning £20,000, 'a 50 per cent gross replacement rate would be equivalent to a 62 per cent net replacement rate'. This varies slightly by income level.

2002, the fourth column assumes that everyone retires when they reach the SPA, the second column is based on calculations that give a greater chance of being in paid work to those who report that they are more likely to remain in paid work, while the third column assumes that those who are currently in paid work retire at the SPA and that those who are currently not in paid work do not return to work.

The first thing to note from Table 6.2 is that even if all those aged between 50 and the SPA (of whom there were 7,446,000 in England in 2002[16]) retired immediately, we predict that once they reached the SPA, only 42.8 per cent of them would have a net replacement rate from pensions alone that was below 67 per cent of their current net income. In other words, the majority (57.2 per cent) would have a net replacement rate from pensions alone that exceeded 67 per cent of their current net income. Turning to the second column, in which each individual is given a probability of remaining in the labour market to the SPA based on their own retirement expectations, we see that over one-in-four individuals (26.9 per cent) are estimated to have total non-owner-occupied-housing wealth worth less than 67 per cent of their pre-retirement income. However, once the value of their other non-pension wealth (including expected inheritances and owner-occupied-housing

Table 6.2
Percentages of individuals predicted to have a net replacement rate of below 67% and below 80% when they reach the SPA

	(1) Retire in 2002	(2) Probabilistic selection of working to SPA	(3) Work to SPA if currently working	(4) Work to SPA
Below 67% net replacement rate				
Pension wealth only	42.8	37.3	27.0	25.1
Non-housing wealth only	31.9	26.9	18.8	17.2
Total wealth	22.2	18.3	13.0	11.5
Total wealth plus expected inheritances	20.4	17.0	12.0	10.6
Total wealth plus expected inheritances plus pension credit	14.0	11.3	8.3	7.9
Below 80% net replacement rate				
Pension wealth only	56.2	51.6	40.9	39.2
Non-housing wealth only	45.5	40.9	31.5	29.9
Total wealth	34.6	30.4	22.8	20.7
Total wealth plus expected inheritances	33.2	29.1	21.5	19.4
Total wealth plus expected inheritances plus pension credit	27.0	23.1	16.6	15.9

Note: Sample size = 4,667.

---

[16] Source: Government Actuary's Department, population figures for England in 2002, http://www.gad.gov.uk/Population/2002/england/weng02singyear.xls.

wealth) is included, this falls to just over one-in-six (17.0 per cent). Potential receipt of the pension credit reduces this even further, to just over one-in-nine individuals (11.3 per cent).

The bottom half of Table 6.2 shows the percentage of individuals predicted to be at risk of having a 'current income net replacement rate' of less than 80 per cent. (On average, this will translate to a gross replacement rate of around 67 per cent.[17]) Again focusing on the second column, in which each individual is given a probability of remaining in the labour market to the SPA based on their own retirement expectations, we see that 40.9 per cent of individuals are estimated to have total non-owner-occupied-housing wealth worth less than 80 per cent of their pre-retirement income. Once the value of their non-pension wealth (including expected inheritances and owner-occupied-housing wealth) is included, this falls to 29.1 per cent of individuals. Potential receipt of the pension credit reduces this even further, to just under one-in-four individuals (23.1 per cent). It is also important to recall that, to the extent to which individuals remaining in paid work choose to increase their future pension contributions or save at all in non-pension forms, these figures will *overstate* the actual numbers reaching the SPA with a replacement rate below these benchmark levels (although some individuals may reduce their pension contribution rate and/or run down their non-pension wealth before the SPA, which could lead to these figures being underestimates).

It is clear from Table 6.2 that relatively few individuals will have retirement resources worth less than 67 per cent of their current net income. However, there are a reasonable number of people whose retirement resources look likely to be between 67 and 80 per cent of their current net income. This raises the question of which threshold, if any, is a better benchmark for 'adequacy'. Using data from the British Retirement Survey, Blundell and Tanner (1999) examine the incomes in 1994 of men who were aged 60–64 and in paid work in 1988–89. They find evidence of considerable variation in average net replacement rates by income: among those in the poorest quintile of the income distribution in 1988–89, average replacement rates were 74 per cent, while among the richest quintile, they were 56 per cent. This might suggest that the 67 per cent replacement rate is a sensible one on which to focus. However, it should also be noted that the Blundell and Tanner calculations only include income and not other retirement resources (such as net financial wealth or housing wealth). This might suggest that a higher threshold, such as 80 per cent, is indeed more appropriate.

6.1.3 An alternative income-related interpretation of adequacy

Partly as a result of the evidence from Blundell and Tanner (1999), the interim report by the Pensions Commission presented estimates of saving adequacy using an assumed replacement rate that varied with individuals' earnings.[18] The definition of replacement rate that it examined was the gross amount of income as a percentage of current gross earnings. As such, the measure is only relevant for those

---

[17] Paragraph 3 of annex 4 of Department for Work and Pensions (2002) states that for an individual earning £20,000, 'a two-thirds gross replacement rate would be equivalent to a net replacement rate of nearly 80 per cent'. This varies slightly by income level. See also figure 4.6, page 135, of Pensions Commission (2004).
[18] See chapter 4 of Pensions Commission (2004).

Table 6.3
Replacement rates assumed in recent Pensions Commission analysis

Gross income	Assumed *gross* replacement rate
Less than £9,500	80%
£9,500 to £17,499	70%
£17,500 to £24,999	67%
£25,000 to £39,999	60%
£40,000 and over	50%

Source: Table G.1, page 169, appendix G of Pensions Commission (2004). Oliver, Wyman & Company (2001) also chose differential replacement rate targets based on current income level.

who are currently in paid work. Table 6.3 sets out the replacement rates that the Pensions Commission chose for each earnings band. Middle earners (those on between £17,500 and £24,999) were assumed to require at least a 67 per cent gross replacement rate (which is consistent with the 80 per cent net replacement rate analysis presented in Section 6.1.2). Lower earners were deemed to require a greater replacement rate to have an adequate retirement income. In contrast, higher earners were assumed to require a lower gross replacement rate to provide an adequate income. For example, those earning £40,000 a year or more were assumed to require a gross replacement rate of 50 per cent (which is roughly equivalent to the 67 per cent net replacement rate analysis presented in Section 6.1.2).

Table 6.4 shows the percentage of individuals predicted to be at risk of having a gross replacement rate of less than that assumed to be required for an adequate retirement income in the Pensions Commission interim report (as set out in Table 6.3). Again, we find that a majority (54.0 per cent) of those aged between 50 and the SPA would, at the SPA, have an income above this benchmark adequacy level even if they left the labour market immediately and relied solely on their pension(s) to provide resources in their retirement.

Table 6.4
Percentage of individuals in families with employment income predicted to have replacement rate below Pensions Commission benchmark when they reach the SPA

	(1) Retire in 2002	(2) Probabilistic selection of working to SPA	(3) Work to SPA if currently working	(4) Work to SPA
Pension wealth only	46.0	38.8	26.1	25.3
Non-housing wealth only	35.1	29.1	18.5	17.8
Total wealth	23.1	18.3	10.5	10.0
Total wealth plus expected inheritances	20.8	16.2	9.0	8.7
Total wealth plus expected inheritances plus pension credit	16.5	12.6	7.4	7.3

Note: Sample size = 3,605.

We also find that a small, but not insignificant, number of individuals aged between 50 and the SPA are at risk of falling below this benchmark for adequacy. Focusing on the second column, in which each individual is given a probability of remaining in the labour market to the SPA based on their own retirement expectations, and taking all wealth (including owner-occupied-housing wealth and expected receipt of inheritances), we see that 16.2 per cent of individuals currently in paid work are at risk of having resources worth less than their benchmark. This is equivalent to just under 940,000 individuals aged between 50 and the SPA in England. Including potential receipt of the pension credit reduces the number significantly. This is not surprising, given that it is those on lower earnings who are assumed to require a higher replacement rate and are also more likely to qualify for the pension credit. We find that just one-in-eight (12.6 per cent) of those currently in paid work would then have retirement resources worth less than the Pensions Commission assumed benchmark replacement rate. This is equivalent to 730,000 individuals in England aged between 50 and the SPA. Again, it is important to recall that, to the extent to which individuals remaining in paid work choose to increase their future pension contributions or save at all in non-pension forms, these figures will *overstate* the actual numbers reaching the SPA with a replacement rate below these benchmark levels. Despite this, these figures are much smaller than those found by the Pensions Commission analysis. It estimates that across the whole UK, depending on when individuals began their retirement saving, there are between 1.6 and 1.8 million people aged between 56 and the SPA, and a further 3.3 to 3.8 million individuals aged between 46 and 55, who are under-saving.[19]

The proportion of the population that we predict will have retirement resources worth less than the Pensions Commission benchmark is significantly lower than the numbers that the Pensions Commission's interim report suggested would be below its benchmark. Pensions Commission (2004) estimated that between 38 and 43 per cent of all individuals in the UK aged between 46 and the SPA had inadequate resources to reach the benchmark replacement rates. In contrast, we estimate that between just 12.6 and 38.8 per cent of employed individuals in England aged between 50 and the SPA will have resources worth less than the Pensions Commission benchmark when they reach the SPA. This equates to between 9.8 and 30.2 per cent of all individuals in England aged between 50 and the SPA.

There are a number of reasons why our estimates differ from those made by the Pensions Commission. The two main reasons are described here. First, the Pensions Commission only looked at individuals' pension wealth. Table 6.4 shows that, if we look exclusively at pension wealth, the proportion of individuals predicted to be at risk is far higher than if we also include other resources that individuals could use to fund their retirement consumption. Second, the Pensions Commission considered all individuals separately, rather than as family units as we do. As a result of this, the Pensions Commission deemed that a low-income individual (earning, say, £5,000) married to a high-income individual (earning, say, £35,000) needs to achieve 80 per cent replacement of their own income, while their partner needs to achieve 60 per cent replacement of their own income. In contrast, we regard the family as being collectively high-income (since total family earned income is £40,000) and so consider that it requires 50 per cent replacement of earned income in retirement.

---

[19] See figures 4.16 and 4.17, page 161, of Pensions Commission (2004).

Thus we would find fewer people at risk even if we were using the same figures for wealth as the Pensions Commission used.

6.1.4 How far below 'adequate' are incomes predicted to be?

The previous analysis has described the proportion of individuals who are likely to have inadequate resources, under different measures of inadequacy. But we have, as yet, given no indication of how near individuals are to these adequacy benchmarks. Since, as already explained, any definition of adequacy is somewhat arbitrary, it is useful to know whether making a slight change to the definition would significantly change the number of people deemed to be at risk.

The potential importance of individual heterogeneity means that each person may well have a different level of income they would like in retirement relative to the income they have before retirement. Therefore the people who are observed to have replacement rates much higher than 67 per cent or 80 per cent have not necessarily behaved suboptimally. Furthermore, since the denominator used in calculating these replacement rates is current net income, if this does not reflect lifetime income then the replacement rate indicated here will also not truly reflect the extent to which retirement income will replace lifetime income. Unfortunately, we do not have a measure of individuals' lifetime incomes, so the replacement rates described in this chapter are the best approximation we have.

Figure 6.2 shows the distribution of net replacement rates under alternative retirement assumptions. Choosing, for example, a 70 per cent replacement rate, the point where each distribution intersects the 70 per cent line indicates the fraction of the population with a replacement rate below 70 per cent. For the probabilistic retirement scenario, this corresponds to 13.8 per cent of individuals aged between 50 and the SPA, whereas for the baseline simulation, it corresponds to 9.9 per cent.

Figure 6.2 thus also shows what proportion of individuals would be deemed at risk were we to have chosen an alternative replacement rate to define adequacy. For example, had we chosen a 50 per cent replacement rate to define adequacy, under the probabilistic retirement scenario 3.5 per cent of individuals would be at risk of having inadequate income in retirement. It is clear from Figure 6.2 that there are many individuals with replacement rates close to the 67 per cent and 80 per cent adequacy lines we have chosen – 25.5 per cent of individuals (under the probabilistic scenario) have predicted replacement rates between 60 and 90 per cent. Therefore, changing the definition of adequacy used does significantly affect the numbers deemed to be at risk.

Figure 6.2 also shows the effect of altering the retirement assumptions on the numbers who are at risk. If we assume that everyone works until the SPA (rather than assuming that their individual expectations of retirement are, on average, what will happen), the percentage of individuals who are predicted to have replacement rates below 90 per cent is 8.2 percentage points lower.

Figure 6.3 shows the distribution of the percentage point difference between the predicted replacement rate and the adequacy benchmark under the three alternative measures of adequacy. Each of these is drawn assuming the probabilistic retirement scenario described above and taking into account housing wealth, inheritances and the pension credit (i.e. the final row in column 2 in Tables 6.1, 6.2 and 6.4). The

Figure 6.2
Distribution of predicted replacement rates under alternative retirement assumptions

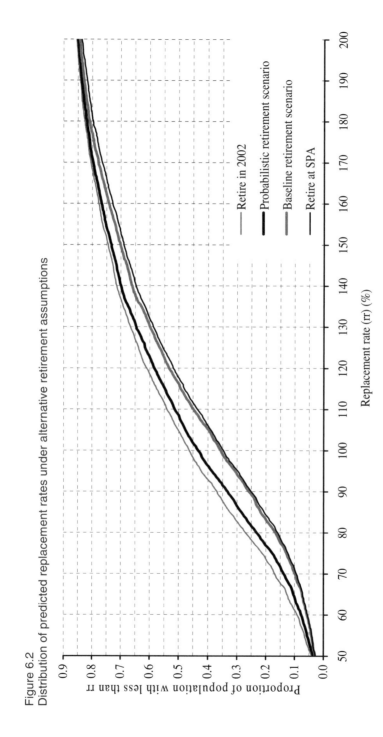

Notes: Replacement rates used are net family retirement income as a percentage of current net total family income. They include all forms of wealth, inheritances and pension credit.

Figure 6.3
Distribution of predicted replacement rates relative to different adequacy benchmarks

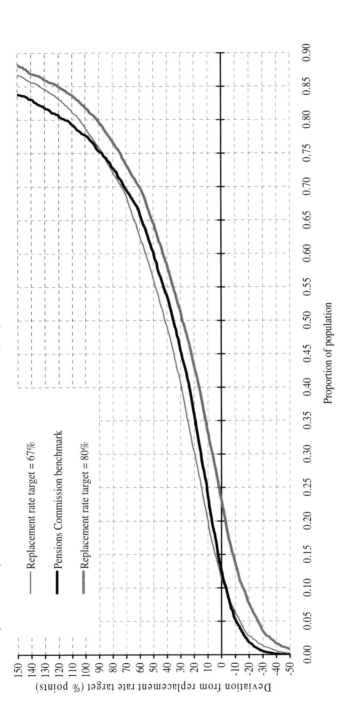

point at which each curve crosses the horizontal axis shows the proportion of those aged between 50 and the SPA who are predicted to have replacement rates at or below the target level. In the case of the Pensions Commission benchmark, the target replacement rate varies with current income, as described in Section 6.1.3.

Again, we see that changing the definition of adequacy slightly will change the proportion of individuals deemed to be at risk. If we reduced the replacement rate deemed adequate by 5 percentage points relative to the Pensions Commission benchmark (for individuals of all income levels), 4.1 per cent fewer currently employed individuals[20] would be classified as at risk. Similarly, if we increased the replacement rate deemed adequate by 5 percentage points, 5.6 per cent more employed individuals would be classified as at risk.

Another interesting question is what additional income the individuals who are at risk would require in retirement to bring them up to the definition of adequacy. Table 6.5 shows how many individuals are predicted to be at risk under each

Table 6.5

Size of the 'at risk' group and average shortfall amongst those at risk for each measure of inadequacy

Measure of inadequacy	Size of 'at risk' group		Average shortfall		Average additional annual saving required between 2002 and SPA	
	% of individuals aged 50– SPA	Number of individuals aged 50– SPA in England ('000s)	% of current income	£	% of current income	£
Measures applicable to all individuals:						
<PCG	≈0	≈0	≈0	≈0	≈0	≈0
<67% of current net income	11.3	845.0	11.6	3,582	20.2	6,466
<80% of current net income	23.1	1,723.4	12.7	3,420	23.3	5,877
Measure applicable only to individuals in families with earned income:						
<Pensions Commission benchmark	12.6	728.5	8.4	2,345	14.2	4,264

Notes: Average figures refer to median values. This table assumes probabilistic likelihood of remaining in paid work until the SPA and includes income in retirement from the pension credit. Sample size for measures applicable to all individuals = 4,493. Sample size for '<Pensions Commission benchmark' = 3,488 as only applies to those currently in paid work.

---

[20] 'Employed individuals' are any individuals whose family received some income from working.

definition of adequacy and the average shortfall amongst the 'at risk' groups. The second row of the table shows that, amongst the 11.3 per cent of individuals aged between 50 and the SPA who are predicted to have replacement rates below 67 per cent, the median shortfall is 11.6 per cent of current income. In other words, the median predicted replacement rate amongst this group is 55.4 per cent. On average, these individuals would require an additional £3,582 a year of income in retirement to provide them with a 67 per cent replacement rate. If we use the 80 per cent replacement rate definition of adequacy, individuals would on average require an additional £3,420 a year of retirement income to provide them with an 80 per cent replacement rate.

Even though a larger proportion of individuals are predicted to be at risk under the Pensions Commission benchmark than under the 67 per cent replacement rate benchmark, the median shortfall relative to the Pensions Commission benchmark is just 8.4 per cent of current income, indicating that those individuals who are below the Pensions Commission benchmark are not as far below. For this reason (and also because the Pensions Commission benchmark requires that lower-income individuals have higher replacement rates in retirement than higher-income individuals[21]), the average shortfall amongst those at risk under the Pensions Commission benchmark is just £2,345 per year.

The final two columns of Table 6.5 show how much, on average, the individuals in the 'at risk' group would need to save each year (on top of their current private pension contributions, under the probabilistic retirement scenario) between 2002 and reaching the SPA in order to have sufficient resources at the SPA to provide them with the relevant replacement rate throughout their retirement. On average, those at risk of having a replacement rate below 67 per cent will need to save an additional £6,466 a year between 2002 and reaching the SPA in order to have sufficient resources at retirement to provide them with 67 per cent replacement of current net income. Equivalently, this group would need, on average, to save an additional 20.2 per cent of their current income each year between 2002 and the SPA. However, this is under the probabilistic retirement assumption. If, instead, all these individuals work between 2002 and the SPA, the additional saving that would be required each year for this group falls to 11.6 per cent of net current income, or £3,156 a year.

The additional saving required is higher if all individuals want to achieve 80 per cent replacement of current income. If all individuals want to have this level of retirement resources, those currently at risk of falling below this level would need to save an additional 23.3 per cent of their current income each year. Given that this is the additional saving that would be required (on top of the proportion of their current income that they already save each year), it seems unlikely that many of those at risk would be able to make up the shortfall through additional saving alone.

The additional saving required is lower if we look at those at risk of falling below the Pensions Commission benchmark. These individuals would need to save an additional £4,264 (or 14.2 per cent of their earned income) each year until they reach the SPA.

---

[21] In other words, low-income individuals are more likely to be at risk than high-income individuals.

6.2 Expectations of those at risk of having inadequate resources in retirement

Section 6.1 showed that the majority of individuals aged between 50 and the state pension age appear to be well placed to retire on an adequate level of resources in retirement. There are, however, a not insignificant number of individuals whose retirement resources look likely to fall short of the benchmark adequacy levels that we have chosen. The appropriate policy response (if any) is likely to depend on the extent to which those who have low levels of resources to provide for their own retirement are aware of this fact. For example, if those whom we deem to have inadequate resources believe that their retirement resources are sufficient, then this might suggest that greater provision of information or simplification of the pension system could help. Conversely, if individuals whose retirement resources are inadequate have always known this to be the case, then greater financial education would be less likely to be a fruitful exercise. Indeed, in this extreme case, simply allowing these individuals to retire onto 'inadequate' resources might be deemed an acceptable pension policy response. For example, those who expect to retire on inadequate resources might have been reliant on 'inadequate' resources throughout their lifetime, in which case it is not clear whether these individuals would rather have greater resources during retirement or during their working life.

As described in Section 5.3, ELSA respondents are asked 'What are the chances that at some point in the future you will not have enough financial resources to meet your needs?'. It is important to note that individuals could be under- or over-estimating the likelihood that they will not have sufficient financial resources in the future. In particular, the evidence presented in Section 5.2 showing that, on average, individuals appear to be overestimating the amount of private pension income that they will receive could mean that, on average, individuals will be underestimating the likelihood that they will have insufficient financial resources at some point in the future.

In Table 6.6, we present the mean value of this reported chance split by whether or not individuals are predicted to fall short of each of the four benchmarks of adequate resources that were set out in Section 6.1. For each of these benchmarks, we use the probabilistic methodology for determining future labour market participation – that is, individuals who report having a higher chance of being in paid work at older ages are given a higher chance of being in work at the SPA. For each of the benchmarks, we present the mean chances of having inadequate resources for both the scenario where all possible retirement resources are included (i.e. pension wealth, non-pension wealth including owner-occupied-housing wealth, expected inheritances and eligibility for the pension credit) and the one where potential receipt of the pension credit is excluded.

The first row of the table presents evidence from the scenario where we examine whether or not individuals are predicted to have retirement resources worth less than the value of the PCG. On average, those whose resources, excluding the pension credit, are predicted to fall below this threshold report a slightly greater than one-in-two chance (52.4 per cent) of having insufficient financial resources to meet their needs. This is statistically significantly higher than the just over one-in-three (34.0

Table 6.6
Mean expectation (%) of having insufficient resources in the future
by whether or not individual is predicted to have retirement income below
certain 'inadequacy' levels

Measure of inadequacy	All	No pension credit		With pension credit	
		At risk	Not at risk	At risk	Not at risk
Measures applicable to all individuals:					
<PCG	35.4	52.4*	34.0	n/a	n/a
<67% of current net income	35.4	39.8*	34.5	36.5	35.2
<80% of current net income	35.4	38.7*	34.0	36.8	35.0
Measure applicable only to individuals in families with earned income:					
<Pensions Commission benchmark	35.0	41.9*	33.7	40.4*	34.3

Notes: Assumes probabilistic likelihood of remaining in employment until the SPA. Sample size for measures
applicable to all individuals = 4,493. Sample size for '<Pensions Commission benchmark' = 3,488 as only
applies to those currently in paid work. * signifies statistically significant difference at the 95 per cent
confidence level.

per cent) chance reported on average among those whose resources, excluding the
pension credit, are predicted to be at or above this level.

The second and third rows of Table 6.6 present equivalent figures for those for
whom this measure of retirement resources is predicted to fall short of 67 per cent
or 80 per cent of their current net income respectively. Again, when we consider
retirement resources without taking potential receipt of the pension credit into
account, those who are predicted to fall short of these benchmarks have a higher
self-reported chance of not having sufficient finances to cover their needs at some
point in the future. However, this difference is less than for the PCG benchmark.
Moreover, once potential receipt of the pension credit is incorporated, there is no
longer a statistically significant difference in the average reported chance of not
having sufficient finances to cover needs.

The last row of Table 6.6 presents the equivalent figures by whether or not
individuals' retirement resources are predicted to fall below the replacement rates
set out in the Pensions Commission report. We find that, on average, those who are
predicted to fall below this threshold report a higher expected chance of not having
sufficient financial resources to cover their needs. This is regardless of whether
resources from the pension credit are included or not.

6.3 Characteristics of those at risk of having inadequate resources in retirement

Section 6.1 has shown that there is a significant group of individuals who are at risk
of having inadequate resources in retirement, whether adequacy is defined relative
to average earnings or relative to an individual's current income. Policymakers may
wish to target the groups who are most at risk, many of whom (as Section 6.2
showed) are not that much more likely to expect to have insufficient resources than

individuals who are not at risk. Therefore this section examines the characteristics of those most at risk of having insufficient resources. The characteristics of the 'at risk' group vary depending on whether we define adequacy relative to average earnings or relative to an individual's current income. Therefore Section 6.3.1 examines the characteristics of individuals who are at risk of having income below the PCG level and then Section 6.3.2 looks at the characteristics of individuals who are at risk of having retirement income falling below the replacement rate adequacy benchmarks.

Throughout this section, we focus on the 'at risk' measures using the probabilistic likelihood of remaining in paid work and including all pension income, other non-housing wealth annuitised at 5.0 per cent and housing wealth annuitised at 2.5 per cent (or 5.0 per cent in Section 6.3.1). The measures used in Section 6.3.1 do not include income from the pension credit, since this would, by definition, only leave the very small number of individuals with negative net total wealth in the 'at risk' group. However, Section 6.3.2 uses 'at risk' measures calculated including income from the pension credit.

6.3.1 Pension credit guarantee benchmark of adequacy

The PCG benchmark of adequacy identifies those individuals who are at risk of having low retirement income in real terms. In many cases, these are the same individuals who were identified as being poor in Chapter 4 when we looked at the characteristics of individuals across the distribution of total wealth. If lifetime-poor individuals were not predicted to be poor in retirement by this measure (and similarly if non-lifetime-poor individuals were predicted to be poor), it might suggest that large numbers of individuals had behaved suboptimally. Table 6.7 examines the personal characteristics of individuals in the 'at risk' and 'not at risk' groups; Table 6.8 looks at the employment status and asset holdings of these two groups.

Table 6.7 shows that individuals with low levels of education and those with low levels of numeracy[22] are more likely to be at risk: 37.3 per cent of individuals aged between 50 and the SPA have no formal qualifications, but these people comprise 68.6 per cent of the 'at risk' group. Education is a reasonably good proxy for lifetime income. Therefore, this result indicates that the lifetime poor are much more likely to be at risk than those who are not lifetime poor. Education is likely to be a causal factor – individuals with low levels of education will have had (on average) more-limited labour market opportunities and lower wages during their working lives and thus will have been less able and less inclined to build up significant retirement resources. Therefore, they are predicted to have low incomes in retirement.

The 'at risk' group are also more likely to be in poor health: 29.1 per cent of the population aged between 50 and the SPA say they have a health condition that limits their daily activities. However, nearly six-in-ten of those at risk (57.7 per cent) have such a condition, compared with less than three-in-ten (26.7 per cent) of those not at risk. As was discussed in Section 4.4, there are various reasons why we

---

[22] Although there is a positive correlation between low education and low numeracy, these groups do not overlap fully.

Table 6.7
Mean personal characteristics of those likely to have retirement resources
worth less than the PCG benchmark (%)

	All	Not at risk	At risk
Education			
Low	37.3	34.6	68.6
Medium	33.6	34.3	25.4
High	29.1	31.0	6.0
Numeracy			
Level 1 (lowest)	10.9	9.2	30.6
Level 2	39.7	39.0	48.7
Level 3	31.8	33.0	16.9
Level 4 (highest)	17.6	18.8	3.7
Person type			
Female	41.1	39.4	61.9
Of which:			
Never married	1.7	1.4	5.5
Widowed	2.0	1.4	8.0
Separated/Divorced	6.1	3.9	32.5
Currently in couple	31.4	32.7	15.8
Male	58.9	60.6	38.1
Of which:			
Single	11.1	10.6	16.5
Currently in couple	47.8	49.9	21.7
Health status			
Health problems	29.1	26.7	57.7
No health problems	70.9	73.3	42.3

Notes: Assumes probabilistic likelihood of remaining in employment until the SPA. Sample size = 4,667.

may observe this correlation between health and wealth. It is possible that this is also a causal factor. In other words, it is possible that less healthy individuals have had more-limited labour market opportunities and lower earnings during their working lives and also had higher healthcare costs than healthy individuals, and as a result they may have been less able to build up significant retirement resources.

Women are more likely than men to be at risk – women comprise just 41.1 per cent of the 50–SPA population but 61.9 per cent of those at risk. However, this aggregate figure masks the fact that it is specific groups of women who are most at risk. Women in couples, as is the case for men in couples, are less likely to be at risk. Single women, on the other hand, are more likely to be at risk. However, those who have never been married or have been widowed make up only a very small proportion of the 50–SPA population (3.7 per cent of the whole 50–SPA population and 13.5 per cent of the 'at risk' group). Therefore, policymakers may have a greater impact on the size of the 'at risk' group if they targeted divorced and separated women, who make up nearly a third (32.5 per cent) of the 'at risk' group. That members of this group are more likely to be at risk could reflect a number of factors. One of these could be divorce laws (either present or historic). If these women are predicted to be poor because divorce settlements left them relatively disadvantaged compared with their former spouses, the appropriate policy response (at least in respect of future cohorts) may be to change divorce laws rather than to change pension provision. Since this cohort of divorced women could have divorced many years ago, it is possible that their current situation reflects historic divorce laws which have since been changed. In this case, future cohorts of divorced women might not be so likely to be at risk because of the new arrangements that have now been put in place. Therefore, whilst measures may be required to deal with the transitory problem of women who were divorced under the old system, further long-term policy changes may not be required. Of course, the other side of this argument is that if, historically, divorce laws have favoured men but current laws no longer do, divorced men in this cohort ought to be relatively better off than the next cohort of divorced men.

As was discussed in Chapters 3 and 4, the group of people who are out of work and aged between 50 and the SPA is comprised of two very different types of people. First, there are wealthy individuals who believe they have already made adequate provision for an extended retirement and therefore choose to retire early. We would not expect these people to be at risk of having retirement incomes below the PCG level. Second, there are poorer individuals who are not in paid work due to limited labour market opportunities but who do not consider themselves to be retired. We would expect this group to be more likely to have low retirement incomes. Table 6.8 divides the sample into three groups by employment status – in work, not in work and self-defined as retired, and not in work but not self-defined as retired. It confirms that those who define themselves as retired are less likely to be at risk, whereas those who are inactive but not retired are more likely to be at risk, of having retirement resources below the level of the PCG: 10.5 per cent of those aged between 50 and the SPA are not in paid work and define themselves as being retired, but these people make up only 4.5 per cent of the 'at risk' group. In contrast, those who are out of work but not retired make up nearly three-in-five (58.1 per cent) of the 'at risk' group but just one-in-five (20.6 per cent) of the 50–SPA population as a whole.

The other characteristics described in Table 6.8 are further indicators of lifetime resources. Those people who own their own home are generally richer than individuals who do not: while over four-in-five (82.0 per cent) of those aged between 50 and the SPA own their own homes, just 15.9 per cent of those at risk do. Similarly, people who have never been a member of a private pension scheme are likely to be those with low levels of lifetime resources: whilst just one-in-five (20.4 per cent) of those who are not at risk have never been a member of a private pension scheme, three-quarters (75.1 per cent) of those who are at risk have never been a member.

Those who are members of a current DB pension scheme are extremely unlikely to be at risk. Just 0.2 per cent of those at risk are currently a member of a DB pension scheme. This should not be interpreted as necessarily implying that DB schemes are more generous than DC pension schemes. Rather, individuals who are members of DB schemes are, on average, higher earners (as was shown in Figure 3.4) and so these people would be expected to be less likely to be at risk.

Table 6.8
Mean employment and asset characteristics of those likely to have
retirement resources worth less than the PCG benchmark (%)

	All	Not at risk	At risk
Employment			
In paid work	69.0	71.6	37.4
Retired	10.5	11.0	4.5
Inactive, not retired	20.6	17.4	58.1
Housing tenure			
Owner-occupier	82.0	87.5	15.9
Not owner-occupier	18.0	12.5	84.1
Pension status			
Ever in private pension	75.3	79.6	24.9
Of which:			
Has a current scheme	50.2	53.5	11.4
Of which:[a]			
DB	21.6	23.4	0.2
Employer DC (no DB)	10.1	10.6	3.9
Non-employer DC only	15.9	16.9	4.6
No current scheme	25.1	26.1	13.5
Of which:			
Receiving income from some/all past pensions	16.4	17.5	3.0
Not receiving income from any past pensions	8.8	8.6	10.5
Never had a private pension	24.7	20.4	75.1
Offered pension by current employer	42.4	44.6	16.4
Of which:			
Has a current employer scheme	30.2	32.5	3.1
Has a current non-employer scheme	3.6	3.7	2.0
Has no current pension	8.6	8.4	11.4

[a] There are also a small number of people (2.5 per cent of the sample) who do not know the type of pension scheme to which they currently belong.
Notes: Assumes probabilistic likelihood of remaining in paid work until the SPA. Sample size = 4,667.

One area of policy debate has been around whether or not individuals should be compelled to join their employer's pension scheme if one is offered.[23] Table 6.8 shows that those who have been offered an employer scheme but do not have a current pension are more likely to be at risk than those who have been offered a pension and have a current pension of some sort. However, those who are offered a pension but do not take one up are a relatively small group (just one-in-nine, 11.4 per cent, of those at risk), so even compelling all these individuals to join their employer scheme would have little effect on the size of the 'at risk' group. Furthermore, Table 6.8 shows that those people who were offered an employer scheme but rejected it in favour of being a member of an alternative (non-employer)

---

[23] See, for example, paragraphs 120–121 of Department for Work and Pensions (2002).

pension are not more likely to be at risk. Compelling these people to join their employer's scheme would be suboptimal if they had in fact chosen to have an alternative pension because it made them better off (for example, the non-employer scheme is likely to offer greater portability which will be important to those who expect to change employer). Moreover, those who were offered the chance to join an employer scheme and did not make alternative arrangements may have done so because they appropriately decided that the individual contribution required was not worth the cost in terms of forgone current consumption.

In general, those who are at risk of having low retirement incomes are the lifetime poor – those with low levels of education and numeracy, those who do not own their own house and those who have never been a member of a private pension scheme. Single women are also more likely to be at risk, particularly women who are divorced or separated.

6.3.2 Replacement rate benchmarks of adequacy

Section 6.3.1 has looked at the characteristics of those people who are at risk of having retirement income below the level of the PCG. These people are predominantly the lifetime poor. However, much of the policy debate has centred on how to enable individuals to have sufficient resources to provide them with a standard of living in retirement comparable to that which they enjoyed before retirement. Therefore policymakers may be interested in identifying those individuals who are most at risk of having significantly lower income in retirement than they currently have, rather than identifying those who are at risk of having low income relative to the rest of the population. This section examines the characteristics of those at risk of having replacement rates below 67 per cent, 80 per cent and the Pensions Commission benchmark rates.

Table 6.9 shows the employment and asset characteristics of those at risk and not at risk of having net retirement income below either 67 per cent or 80 per cent of their current net income. The most important result from this table is that those in paid work are more likely to be at risk. This is because they have higher current incomes and thus require more retirement income to reach the required replacement rate. Those not in paid work will generally be of two types. First, there are those on low incomes, for whom flat-rate state pensions and pension credit payments will replace a large portion of any income they currently have. These people are therefore less likely to have low replacement rates. Table 6.9 shows that those who are not in paid work but not retired are less likely to be at risk (just 9.5 per cent of those at risk of having a replacement rate below 67 per cent are out of work but not retired, compared with 20.6 per cent in the whole 50–SPA population). Second, there are those wealthy individuals who have already retired and who are receiving their private pensions already. For these people, the main change that they are likely to see in their incomes when they reach the SPA is that they will start receiving income from state pensions, in addition to the income from private pensions that they are already receiving. Therefore these people are also likely to have post-SPA income that is a high proportion of their current income. This is confirmed by Table 6.9, which shows that individuals who define themselves as retired are less likely to be at risk (even more so than those individuals who are inactive but not retired) –

Table 6.9
Mean employment and asset characteristics of different groups that could be considered to be at risk of inadequate retirement resources (%)

	All	< 67% replacement rate (11.3%)		< 80% replacement rate (23.1%)	
		Not at risk	At risk	Not at risk	At risk
Employment					
In paid work	69.0	66.6	87.3	63.5	86.9
Retired	10.5	11.4	3.2	12.9	2.5
Inactive, not retired	20.6	22.0	9.5	23.6	10.6
Housing tenure					
Owner-occupier	82.0	82.6	77.5	82.8	79.2
Not owner-occupier	18.0	17.4	22.5	17.2	20.8
Pension status					
Ever in private pension	75.3	75.3	75.7	75.2	76.0
Of which:					
Has a current scheme	50.2	49.3	57.4	47.6	59.0
Of which:[a]					
DB	21.6	22.7	13.2	23.2	16.4
Employer DC (no DB)	10.1	9.2	16.8	8.3	16.3
Non-employer DC only	15.9	15.1	22.3	14.1	22.0
No current scheme	25.1	26.0	18.3	27.6	17.0
Of which:					
Receiving income from some/all past pensions	16.4	17.2	9.5	18.5	9.4
Not receiving income from any past pensions	8.8	8.8	8.8	9.1	7.6
Never had a private pension	24.7	24.7	24.3	24.8	24.0
Offered pension by current employer	42.4	41.8	47.5	40.0	50.3
Of which:					
Has a current employer scheme	30.2	30.3	29.2	29.7	31.8
Has a current non-employer scheme	3.6	3.5	4.2	3.1	5.5
Has no current pension	8.6	7.9	14.1	7.3	13.1

[a] There are also a small number of people (2.5 per cent of the sample) who do not know the type of pension scheme to which they currently belong.
Notes: Assumes probabilistic likelihood of remaining in paid work until the SPA. Sample size = 4,667.

just 3.2 per cent of those at risk of having a replacement rate below 67 per cent are not in paid work and report being retired, compared with 10.5 per cent of the whole 50–SPA population. This is why we observe that individuals in paid work are more likely to be at risk.

Those individuals who are currently members of a private pension scheme are also more likely to be at risk of having low replacement rates. Again, this is because virtually all those who have a current private pension are in paid work and thus have higher incomes to replace. However, amongst those with current pension schemes, DB scheme members are less likely to be at risk, whereas DC scheme members are more likely to be at risk. One reason for this (in the case of those people who are members of non-employer DC schemes) is that people who believe they are at risk of having inadequate resources may take out a DC pension scheme in order to boost their retirement income. In other words, the causality could be that people who are at risk join DC schemes to improve their retirement provision, rather than that individuals in DC schemes are more likely to be at risk than otherwise identical individuals in DB schemes.

One group who have private pensions and who are much less likely to be at risk are those who are currently receiving income from a private pension: 16.4 per cent of individuals aged between 50 and the SPA are not currently members of a private pension but are currently receiving income from a past pension, whereas just 9.5 per cent of those at risk of having a replacement rate below 67 per cent (and 9.4 per cent of those at risk of having a replacement rate below 80 per cent) are in this position. This is not surprising since the majority of these people will already be retired, so their current income should be close to their post-SPA income. For this group, we would ideally want to compare their income at the SPA with some measure of their lifetime income, but (as we have already mentioned) we do not yet have a suitable measure of lifetime income for ELSA respondents. To the extent that this group are under-saving, however, the appropriate initial policy response would probably be to encourage these people to return to work rather than to simply save more.

As we saw in Table 6.8, those people who have been offered the chance to join their employer's pension scheme but have not done so are more likely to be at risk than those who do join. Using the measures of inadequacy used here, it is not just those people who do not join their employer's scheme and have no other private pension, but also those who do not join and do have some other private pension arrangement, who are more likely to be at risk. However, this is still a very small group of people (just 18.3 per cent of those at risk of a replacement rate below 67 per cent and 18.6 per cent of those at risk of a replacement rate below 80 per cent). Therefore, forcing these people to join their employer's pension scheme may not reduce the size of the 'at risk' group very much.

Other things being equal, those with high current incomes are more at risk of having low replacement rates in retirement because they have more income to replace. This means that the individuals who are likely to be at risk of having low replacement rates are not necessarily those who were identified as being at risk when we used the PCG benchmark (in Section 6.3.1). Table 6.10 shows the correlation between the various 'at risk' measures described above. It shows that 4.3 per cent of individuals are predicted to have retirement resources below the level of the PCG *and* below 67 per cent of their current income, while 12.8 per cent of individuals are deemed to be at risk of having a replacement rate below 67 per cent of their current income but are *not* predicted to have retirement resources that will be below the level of the PCG. In other words, only one-in-four (25.2 per cent) of those deemed to be at risk of having a replacement rate below 67 per cent of their current income are also predicted to be at risk of having retirement income below the level of the PCG. Similarly, only 55.6 per cent of those at risk of having resources worth less than the PCG are also at risk of having a replacement rate

Table 6.10
Percentage of individuals 'at risk' under both the pension credit guarantee and replacement rate definitions of adequacy

	Not at risk under either	At risk under PCG definition only	At risk under replacement rate definition only	At risk under both	Unweighted *N*
Measures applicable to all individuals:					
<67% of current net income	79.5	3.4	12.8	4.3	4,667
<80% of current net income	68.5	2.5	23.8	5.2	4,667
Measure applicable only to individuals in families with earned income:					
< Pensions Commission benchmark	82.3	1.6	13.7	2.5	3,605

below 67 per cent. Therefore, the characteristics observed to be associated with being at risk in Table 6.9 are different from those associated with being at risk in Table 6.8. In fact, the characteristics associated with being at risk in Table 6.9 are the same characteristics associated with having high current income – being in paid work and currently being a member of a private pension. As was discussed in Section 6.1, it is possible that the replacement rate that an individual desires in retirement depends on what their pre-retirement income is. Low-income individuals may need income very close to their current income in order to maintain their standard of living, whereas high-income individuals may be happy to have lower replacement rates.

Table 6.11 examines the characteristics associated with being at risk of having a replacement rate below the Pensions Commission benchmark rates, which refer to replacement of gross current earnings. Therefore, the group at risk is only defined for those whose family currently receives some earned income. The characteristics associated with being at risk here differ from those in Table 6.9 for two main reasons. First, this table includes only those in families with some earned income; therefore the issue identified for Table 6.9 that those in paid work are more likely to be at risk simply because they have higher current incomes does not apply here. Second, this definition of adequacy allows that high-income individuals need to replace a lower fraction of their income than low-income individuals.

Individuals who have ever had a private pension are less likely to be at risk – this applies whether they are currently a member of a private pension or whether they used to be but no longer are: 82.1 per cent of those not at risk have ever been members of a private pension, compared with 71.4 per cent of those who are at risk. However, current DB scheme members are less likely to be at risk, whereas current DC scheme members are more likely to be at risk. Again, this is probably a reflection of the fact that DB scheme members are higher earners than DC scheme

Table 6.11
Mean employment and asset characteristics of different groups that could be considered to be at risk of inadequate retirement resources (%)

	All	< Pensions Commission benchmark (12.6%)	
		Not at risk	At risk
Housing tenure			
Owner-occupier	87.7	89.7	73.7
Not owner-occupier	12.3	10.3	26.3
Pension status			
Ever in private pension	80.7	82.1	71.4
Of which:			
Has a current scheme	61.9	62.1	60.3
Of which:[a]			
DB	27.6	30.3	8.6
Employer DC (no DB)	12.6	11.7	18.8
Non-employer DC only	18.5	17.4	26.5
No current scheme	18.8	19.9	11.1
Of which:			
Receiving income from some/all past pensions	11.1	12.3	2.4
Not receiving income from any past pensions	7.8	7.6	8.7
Never had a private pension	19.3	17.9	28.6
Offered pension by current employer	54.4	54.5	53.5
Of which:			
Has a current employer scheme	38.7	40.4	27.1
Has a current non-employer scheme	4.6	4.3	7.0
Has no current pension	11.0	9.8	19.5

[a] There are also a small number of people (3.2 per cent of the sample) who do not know the type of pension scheme to which they currently belong.
Notes: Assumes probabilistic likelihood of remaining in paid work until the SPA. Sample size = 3,605.

members and so are required to replace a lower fraction of their earnings in order to avoid being classed as at risk.

In Table 6.9, because not having a private pension is correlated with not being in paid work, we saw that those who had never been a member of a private pension were marginally less likely to be at risk. However, Table 6.11 (which concentrates just on those with some earned income) shows that those who have never been a member of a private pension are much more likely to be at risk. They comprise just under one-in-five (19.3 per cent) of those individuals with some earned income but nearly three-in-ten of those at risk (28.6 per cent). Those who have been offered a pension by their employer but chose not to join it or any other pension scheme (some of whom will also never have been a member of a private pension) are also more likely to be at risk. These people now comprise nearly a fifth (19.5 per cent) of those at risk.

The 67 per cent and 80 per cent replacement rate definitions of adequacy used in this chapter are based on individuals having to replace some part of their existing income. As a result, those who are in paid work (i.e. on average have higher incomes) are more likely to be at risk than those who are not in paid work. Therefore, it would be useful to examine the characteristics of 'at risk' individuals separately for those who are in paid work and those who are not. This also allows us to compare these working 'at risk' groups and the 'at risk' group using the Pensions Commission adequacy benchmark.[24] Table 6.12 presents the results of a multivariate analysis of the characteristics of working individuals defined as being at risk under each of the three replacement rate adequacy benchmarks. Since many of the characteristics that are included in Table 6.12 are correlated with one another – for example, education level and numeracy – using a multivariate analysis allows us to distinguish which are individually significant in identifying the 'at risk' group.

The first two columns of Table 6.12 report the odds of being at risk, given certain characteristics, using benchmarks of adequacy defined as having to replace either 67 per cent or 80 per cent of all current income. An odds ratio of 1 means that the characteristic is not associated with a higher or lower chance of being at risk. An odds ratio of greater than 1 indicates that the characteristic is associated with a greater chance of being at risk (and vice versa). The third column reports the odds of being at risk, given certain characteristics, using a replacement rate benchmark that varies by the level of current earnings and requires only that current earned

Table 6.12
Association between personal characteristics and whether considered to be at risk of inadequate retirement resources (those currently in paid work only)

	< 67% replacement rate	< 80% replacement rate	< Pensions Commission benchmark
	Odds ratio	Odds ratio	Odds ratio
Age	0.99	0.97	0.95*
Low education	0.83	0.90	1.53*
Mid education	0.94	0.97	1.50*
Female, never married	0.49	0.88	1.03
Female, widowed	1.42	1.24	0.58
Female, separated/divorced	1.59*	1.13	3.06*
Female, couple	0.97	0.84*	0.77*
Male, single	1.65*	1.91*	3.37*
Has limiting health problems	0.86	0.94	1.02
Numeracy level 1 (low)	0.95	1.28	1.49
Numeracy level 2	1.02	1.22	1.45*
Numeracy level 3	1.01	1.08	1.06

Notes: Assumes probabilistic likelihood of remaining in paid work until the SPA. Sample size = 3,118. The base group is men in couples with a degree, no health problem and high numeracy. * signifies statistically significant difference at the 95 per cent confidence level.

---

[24] Since the Pensions Commission benchmark is based on replacement of earned income, only individuals who are in paid work and their partners can be deemed to be at risk or not using the Pensions Commission benchmark.

income, not total current income, is replaced. The measure of what has to be replaced is important in determining who is identified as at risk by each benchmark. In particular, individuals who currently have high unearned income (which they will continue to receive beyond the SPA) relative to their earned income will find it easier to achieve a high replacement rate under the Pensions Commission definition because their unearned income will be deemed to 'replace' their earned income, even though they already receive this income. This is why, for example, Table 6.12 shows that widows (who in many instances will be in receipt of a widow's pension) are 42 per cent more likely than working men in couples to be at risk using the 67 per cent replacement rate definition but 42 per cent less likely to be at risk using the Pensions Commission benchmark (though neither of these differences is statistically significant at conventional levels).

The first two columns of Table 6.12 show that very few factors are associated with significantly higher chances of being at risk of having replacement rates of 67 or 80 per cent, whereas the third column shows that many more characteristics are significantly associated with being below the Pensions Commission benchmark. This is because in the first two columns (where a flat replacement rate definition of adequacy is used), there are two different groups who may be at risk – wealthy individuals, who will have higher incomes in retirement but also have more current income to replace, and poorer individuals, who will have less income in retirement but also lower current incomes to replace. As a result, virtually none of these personal characteristics are significantly associated with being at risk because the characteristics of these rich and poor individuals are different.

Some characteristics are significantly associated with higher chances of being at risk amongst working individuals using the 67 and 80 per cent replacement rate benchmarks. Divorced women who are in paid work are 59 per cent more likely to have a replacement rate below 67 per cent (and 13 per cent more likely to have a replacement rate below 80 per cent, although this difference is not statistically significant) than working men in couples. Similarly, single men are much more likely than men in couples to have low replacement rates – they are 65 per cent more likely to have a replacement rate below 67 per cent and 91 per cent more likely to have a replacement rate below 80 per cent than men in couples.

If we look at the Pensions Commission benchmark, which requires poor individuals to achieve a higher replacement rate than rich individuals, many more personal characteristics are significantly associated with being at risk. Individuals with lower levels of education and those with lower levels of numeracy (conditional on education) are more likely to be at risk. Compared with those with degree-level qualifications, those with qualifications below degree level are 50 per cent more likely to be at risk.

Using this definition, we also find that working divorced women and single men are very much more likely to be at risk than working men in couples (206 per cent and 237 per cent more likely, respectively). However, women in couples who are working are 23 per cent less likely to be at risk than men in couples who are working.

So far, we have only looked at the characteristics of those individuals who are in paid work and at risk. The characteristics of those who are not in paid work and at risk may be very different from these. Table 6.13 shows the results of multivariate

Table 6.13
Association between personal characteristics and whether considered to be at risk of inadequate retirement resources (those not currently in paid work only)

	< 67% replacement rate Odds ratio	< 80% replacement rate Odds ratio
Age	1.01	0.99
Low education	1.57	1.52
Mid education	1.68	1.41
Female, never married	2.43	1.43
Female, widowed	0.54	0.76
Female, separated/divorced	1.18	0.89
Female, couple	1.43	1.71*
Male, single	0.59	0.64
Has limiting health problems	1.75*	1.94*
Numeracy level 1 (low)	1.12	1.26
Numeracy level 2	0.70	0.96
Numeracy level 3	0.96	1.14

Notes: Assuming probabilistic likelihood of being in paid work until the SPA. Sample size = 1,549. The base group is men in couples with a degree, no health problem and high numeracy. * signifies statistically significant difference at the 95 per cent confidence level.

analysis of the characteristics of those at risk of replacement rates below 67 per cent and below 80 per cent.

Table 6.12 showed that working individuals who have a health problem are no more likely to be at risk than working individuals without a health problem. However, Table 6.13 shows that amongst those individuals who are not in work, those with health problems are significantly more likely to be at risk of having low replacement rates in retirement. Individuals with health problems are 75 per cent more likely to have a replacement rate below 67 per cent and 94 per cent more likely to have a replacement rate below 80 per cent than individuals who do not have a health problem. This suggests that it is not just having any health problem that makes individuals more at risk, but rather that it is having a health condition that means an individual is out of the labour market that is important. This group may be of particular concern to policymakers since economically inactive individuals in poor health are much less likely to expect to be in work in future than economically inactive healthy individuals.[25]

Overall, Table 6.13 shows that those out-of-work individuals who are least likely to be at risk of having low replacement rates are highly educated men. These are a group of people who we would typically expect to have the greatest labour market opportunities. The fact that these people are out of work prior to the SPA therefore suggests that they have chosen to retire early because they believe their retirement provision is adequate. Consequently, it is not surprising that these individuals are unlikely to be at risk of having low replacement rates.

---

[25] Banks and Casanova, 2003.

This section has shown that the groups identified as being at risk by the universal 67 per cent and 80 per cent replacement rate adequacy thresholds (which measure the replacement of all current income) are somewhat different from the groups identified as being at risk by the Pensions Commission adequacy threshold (which refers only to the replacement of earned income and varies by income level).[26] Working individuals are more likely to be at risk of having replacement rates below 67 per cent or 80 per cent because they are more likely to have high current incomes and hence have more income to replace. Amongst working individuals, divorced women and single men are more likely to be at risk according to all measures. Amongst those out of work, those most likely to be at risk of having replacement rates below 67 per cent or 80 per cent are individuals with health problems, whereas those least likely to be at risk are men with high levels of education.

That so few personal characteristics are significantly associated with being more at risk of having a low replacement rate is itself an important finding. Section 6.3.1 showed that there are certain groups (such as those with fewer years of formal education) who are much more likely to have income below the PCG level, which means that it is possible to target policies on those most at risk of income poverty in retirement. In contrast, those who are at risk of having low replacement rates are a very heterogeneous group who cannot, prior to their retirement, be easily identified from data on their characteristics alone. Even if the government observed all the personal characteristics described in Tables 6.12 and 6.13 (including each individual's level of numeracy), it would be very difficult to target policies accurately on those most at risk. As a result, any policy that attempted to increase the replacement rates of those currently approaching retirement would be likely to have a large deadweight loss. In other words, whilst government intervention to help ensure future pensioners avoid income poverty can be well targeted, government intervention to increase the adequacy of retirement incomes (in terms of replacing a reasonable proportion of pre-retirement income) is likely to be focused imprecisely.[27]

---

[26] This, in turn, leads to questions about which, if any, might be the appropriate way to measure 'adequacy'.

[27] For example, the 1998 Green Paper (Department for Work and Pensions, 1998) targeted stakeholder pensions at middle earners (those earning between £9,000 and £18,500 a year) who did not have a private pension since it was believed that this was a group who should be encouraged to make greater retirement provision. However, subsequent analysis showed that a large majority of people in this earnings band already had a private pension, and that those who did not were less likely to have stable employment and earnings, and more likely to have lower levels of saving (Disney, Emmerson and Tanner, 1999).

CHAPTER 7
Conclusions

This report has provided new empirical evidence on the retirement saving arrangements of individuals aged between 50 and the state pension age (SPA) in England. Using detailed data on pension arrangements from the English Longitudinal Study of Ageing, we have been able to estimate pension wealth (and future pension incomes) in order to add them to measures of financial, housing and other wealth.

Our results reveal a number of broad patterns in the data. As anticipated, the distribution of retirement wealth is very unequal, although the inequality is different for the various components, with state pension wealth being relatively equally distributed across the population, as would be expected given the nature of the pension system in the UK. More importantly, perhaps, the various forms of wealth do not offset each other – rather than those with low pension wealth having other assets to fund their retirement, they tend to have lower levels of other assets as well. Whilst we find some evidence that the poorer groups do, on average, expect to live for less long than their richer counterparts, this is not enough to change the assessment of their retirement resources, particularly since much of their retirement resources will be annuitised.

An important question that is frequently discussed is whether or not the resources that individuals have for their retirement are 'adequate'. As discussed in Chapter 6, defining what is meant by 'adequate' is not straightforward, but our assessment is that there is a small, but not insignificant, group of the population approaching retirement who do appear likely to have retirement resources that fall below commonly used benchmarks of adequacy as they retire over the next 10–15 years. The precise number that fall into this group depends on which benchmark is used. Taking an absolute income measure as a benchmark for adequacy, we find that 7.7 per cent of individuals aged between 50 and the SPA have retirement resources (ignoring means-tested benefits) that would yield incomes below the level of the pension credit guarantee – implicitly the level that the government regards as the minimum amount that pensioners should live on. (They will, of course, be brought up to at least that level if they subsequently take up the means-tested benefits to which they are entitled.) This group is made up of individuals with low levels of total wealth, but these individuals are not the only ones about whom policymakers might be concerned. An alternative way to measure inadequacy is to define it relative to an individual's pre-retirement income. Of course, how high one might wish retirement income to be relative to pre-retirement income is an open question. We find that (including potential entitlement to pension credit) 11.3 per cent of individuals aged between 50 and the SPA will experience income during retirement that is less than 67 per cent of pre-retirement income, but this proportion rises to 23.1 per cent if we define inadequacy as being retirement income that is less than 80 per cent of pre-retirement income. If one is willing to make more restrictive assumptions about individuals' (un)willingness to use housing wealth to finance retirement consumption, this group will be larger.

As well as generating different numbers at risk, we show that the two alternative approaches to defining adequacy – targeting either an absolute low level of retirement income or else low retirement income relative to that in work – also suggest different types of individuals at risk. Those at risk of inadequate resources under both definitions are a rather small subset of the total at risk under either one alone. Essentially, many of those predicted to have low replacement rates are richer individuals with high current earnings/income, whilst those predicted to have low levels of retirement income are much poorer. While the use of the income-specific replacement rate benchmarks adopted by the Pensions Commission goes some way to addressing this, the fundamental issue remains. The dual nature of the pension system (taking public and private together) – providing poverty alleviation for older individuals at the bottom end of the lifetime income distribution, and income replacement for those further up – is well known, of course, and it is this duality that underpins the fact that both types of benchmarks are discussed in the policy debate. But the relative lack of correspondence between those at risk under each measure just serves to re-emphasise that policymakers need to specify what the pension system is being designed to do before the appropriate targeting of policy (and hence the setting of benchmarks by which policy can be evaluated) can take place.

Finally, we find that people who we would predict to be towards the bottom of the distribution of retirement income when they retire are more likely to report high chances of having 'inadequate retirement resources to meet their needs'. This suggests that there is at least some extent to which individuals are aware of their financial situation. Further attempts to increase retirement saving, if they are to be effective, would have to make such individuals cut their current consumption (which may already be relatively low). Such changes may be harder to induce if individuals are already forgoing retirement saving in the knowledge that their retirement resources will be 'low'.

This microdata-based approach to investigating the 'adequacy' of retirement saving has a number of advantages over aggregate measures, most importantly that the diversity of individual circumstances can, to some extent, be accounted for, and that distributional issues can be investigated. Nevertheless, there are a number of other factors to bear in mind when interpreting our analysis, some of which are related to the points discussed briefly above.

First, there is no sense in which we have assessed whether individuals' situations are 'suboptimal', in the sense of assessing whether a rational economic agent would have ended up saving a different amount from that which we observe in our data. Such a calculation would be very complex – depending on a raft of individual circumstances, expectations and (unknown) preference parameters. Nevertheless, it would be a worthwhile topic for future research, particularly since it would inform the policy debate regarding the balance between reforms based on encouraging voluntary retirement saving (such as information provision, tax incentives and financial education) and reforms increasing further compulsion in retirement saving over and above that already implicitly present in state pensions.

Second, we have said nothing about the retirement saving of those currently under the age of 50. Since this age group is not included in our analysis, we can conclude relatively little about the policy lessons to be learnt for it. Even were such individuals included in our analysis, it would be hard to assess the adequacy of retirement saving for them, since so much more of their life circumstances remains unresolved. In a sense, our 'strong' assumptions relating to work expectations, future income growth and future pension contributions would be even harder to maintain for a group with so much more of their working life ahead of them.

There is one tentative conclusion about this group that we can draw, however. The cohorts we study in this report are the first generations to face less-generous pension provision than their predecessors. This downward trend is set to continue, both through reforms to state pensions taking their full effect and through increased longevity placing pressures on the contributions-to-returns ratio for those with DB pensions and on long-term annuity rates for those with DC pensions. As such, other things being equal, unless the younger cohorts arrive at the age of 50 with more private assets, and/or greater (and realisable) expectations of retiring later, than the cohort that we study here, then the inadequacy of retirement resources will be greater than identified here. Unfortunately, given the data available, there is no way of assessing the savings of the younger generations. And even were such data available, we do not have data on today's older individuals when they themselves were younger (i.e. 10 or 20 years ago), which we would need to make the appropriate comparison across cohorts. It is here that policymakers and researchers in the UK really pay for the past unwillingness to invest in the collection of wealth data. Despite the fact that we are now collecting such data, it will be some time, and probably 10 years at least, before we can reliably look at cross-cohort differences in saving behaviour in a meaningful manner.

Finally, it is unlikely that increasing savings alone will be sufficient to mitigate the problems created by the ageing population in the long run, although the extent to which this is true will depend on a number of factors. After all, asset prices, and hence the rate of return on retirement saving, are determined by both the supply of and the demand for assets. In a closed economy, or (more importantly and more realistically) in an open economy with the majority of the rest of the world facing broadly synchronised demographic projections, the return on assets will fall if savings increase as the population ages. The only question is by how much. The implications of this are now being discussed explicitly in the policy debate. Whilst it may not be an issue for generations currently approaching retirement, it will become an issue in the medium term as the 'baby boomers' move through their retirement, i.e. it will be particularly important for those currently under 50 who we discussed briefly above.

Put differently, as life expectancies increase and the population ages, if retirement ages stay the same then the ratio of workers to non-workers in the economy will fall. This will happen even more rapidly if the fraction of young adults going into higher education continues to increase. Unless the economic fundamentals (i.e. the relative number of productive people in the economy or the average productivity of workers) change, then outcomes, in a first-order sense, will not differ across policy regimes. All that will happen is that relative prices, and therefore the incidence of the burden of the transition across different groups of individuals, will change. It is in this sense that the 'funding problem' inherent in public pensions is still present in private funded pension systems such as that in the UK.

Consequently, it is likely to be increasing labour market participation of future older individuals, as opposed to increased retirement saving of current younger individuals, that will hold the key to a successful economic negotiation of the long-run demographic transition associated with the ageing population. This, in turn, will depend on the balance between labour supply and labour demand for future older workers. In short, future generations will need to expect to work to later ages than their predecessors and will need to be given the opportunity to work to later ages so that their expectations can be fulfilled.

So there is still much research to be done, both on this age group and on younger individuals. Survey measurement technology (particularly for financial variables, expectations and pensions) is improving all the time, and more data are gradually becoming available for analysis. In addition to the future waves of ELSA, the 2005 wave of the British Household Panel Survey and the new ONS Wealth and Assets Survey (planned for 2006–07) will offer good opportunities for further descriptive and econometric analysis for both older and younger groups of the population. With regard to the group we study here, the natural next steps would be to look at how circumstances will change over the years between now and retirement, and to investigate how actual retirement and pension outcomes will differ relative to individuals' current expectations. Given the importance of the policy questions, and the potential diversity of circumstances in the population identified here, such research must be considered critical for the operation of future government policy on retirement and pension saving.

References

Attanasio, O., Banks, J., Blundell, R., Chote, R. and Emmerson, C. (2004), *Pensions, Pensioners and Pensions Policy: Financial Security in UK Retirement Savings?*, IFS Briefing Note no. 48, http://www.ifs.org.uk/publications.php?publication_id=1796.

Attanasio, O. and Emmerson, C. (2003), 'Mortality, health status and wealth', *Journal of the European Economics Association*, vol. 1, pp. 821–50.

Banks, J. and Blundell, R. (2005), 'Private pension arrangements and retirement in Britain', *Fiscal Studies*, vol. 26, pp. 35–53.

Banks, J., Blundell, R. and Emmerson, C. (2005), 'The balance between defined benefit, defined contribution and state provision', *Journal of the European Economic Association*, vol. 3, pp. 466–76.

Banks, J. and Casanova, M. (2003), 'Work and retirement', in M. Marmot, J. Banks, R. Blundell, C. Lessof and J. Nazroo (eds), *Health, Wealth and Lifestyles of the Older Population in England: The 2002 English Longitudinal Study of Ageing*, London: IFS (http://www.ifs.org.uk/elsa/report_wave1.php).

Banks, J., Emmerson, C. and Oldfield, Z. (2004), 'Not so brief lives: longevity expectations and well-being in retirement', in *Seven Ages of Man and Woman: A Look at Life in Britain in the Second Elizabethan Era*, Swindon: Economic and Social Research Council (http://www.ifs.org.uk/publications.php?publication_id=3177).

Banks, J., Emmerson, C. and Oldfield, Z. (2005), 'Preparing for retirement: the pension arrangements and retirement expectations of those approaching state pension age in England', IFS Working Paper no. 05/13, http://www.ifs.org.uk/publications.php?publication_id=3396.

Banks, J., Emmerson, C. and Tetlow, G. (2005), 'Estimating pension wealth of ELSA respondents', IFS Working Paper no. 05/09, http://www.ifs.org.uk/publications.php?publication_id=3369.

Banks, J., Karlsen, S. and Oldfield, Z. (2003), 'Socio-economic position', in M. Marmot, J. Banks, R. Blundell, C. Lessof and J. Nazroo (eds), *Health, Wealth and Lifestyles of the Older Population in England: The 2002 English Longitudinal Study of Ageing*, London: IFS (http://www.ifs.org.uk/elsa/report_wave1.php).

Banks, J., Smith, Z. and Wakefield, M. (2002), 'The distribution of financial wealth in the UK: evidence from 2000 BHPS data', IFS Working Paper no. W02/21, http://www.ifs.org.uk/publications.php?publication_id=1996.

Banks, J. and Tanner, S. (1999), *Household Saving in the UK*, London: IFS (http://www.ifs.org.uk/comms/hhs.pdf).

Blundell, R., Meghir, C. and Smith, S. (2002), 'Pension incentives and the pattern of early retirement', *Economic Journal*, vol. 112, pp. C153–70.

Blundell, R. and Tanner, S. (1999), 'Labour force participation and retirement in the UK', paper prepared for National Academy of Science, mimeo, IFS, http://www.ifs.org.uk/publications.php?publication_id=3432.

Clark, T. and Emmerson, C. (2003), 'Privatising provision and attacking poverty? The direction of UK pension policy under New Labour', *Journal of Pension Economics and Finance*, vol. 2, pp. 67–89.

Department of Social Security (1998), *A New Contract for Welfare: Partnership in Pensions*, Cm. 4179, London: DSS (http://www.dwp.gov.uk/publications/dss/1998/pengp/pdfs/pensions.pdf).

Department for Work and Pensions (2002), *Simplicity, Security and Choice: Working and Saving for Retirement*, Cm. 5677, London: The Stationery Office (http://www.dwp.gov.uk/consultations/consult/2002/pensions/gp.pdf).

Disney, R. and Emmerson, C. (2005), 'Public pension reform in the United Kingdom: what effect on the financial well-being of current and future pensioners?', *Fiscal Studies*, vol. 26, pp. 55–81.

Disney, R., Emmerson, C. and Tanner, S. (1999), *Partnership in Pensions: An Assessment*, Commentary no. 78, London: IFS (http://www.ifs.org.uk/publications.php?publication_id=1939).

Disney, R., Johnson, P. and Stears, G. (1998), 'Asset wealth and asset decumulation among households in the Retirement Survey', *Fiscal Studies*, vol. 19, pp. 153–74.

Emmerson, C., Tetlow, G. and Wakefield, M. (2005), *Pension and Saving Policy*, IFS Election Briefing Note no. 12, http://www.ifs.org.uk/bns/05ebn12.pdf.

Ghilarducci, T. (1992), *Labor's Capital: The Economics and Politics of Private Pensions*, Cambridge, MA: MIT Press.

HM Treasury (2000), *Productivity in the UK: Evidence and the Government's Approach*, London.

Hurd, M. and McGarry, K. (2002), 'The predictive validity of subjective probabilities of survival', *Economic Journal*, vol. 112, pp. 966–85.

Marmot, M., Banks, J., Blundell, R., Lessof, C. and Nazroo, J. (eds) (2003), *Health, Wealth and Lifestyles of the Older Population in England: The 2002 English Longitudinal Study of Ageing*, London: IFS (http://www.ifs.org.uk/elsa/report_wave1.php).

Marmot, M. et al. (2005), *English Longitudinal Study of Ageing (ELSA): Wave 1, 2002–2003* [computer file], 2nd edition, Colchester, Essex: UK Data Archive [distributor], June 2005. SN: 5050.

Oliver, Wyman & Company (2001), *The Future Regulation of UK Savings and Investment*, London. Executive summary is available at http://www.abi.org.uk/oliverwymanreport.pdf.

Pensions Commission (2004), *Pensions: Challenges and Choices. The First Report of the Pensions Commission*, London: The Stationery Office (http://www.pensionscommission.org.uk/publications/2004/annrep/fullreport.pdf).

Poterba, J. and Finkelstein, A. (2002), 'Selection effects in the United Kingdom individual annuities market', *Economic Journal*, vol. 112, pp. 28–50.

Scholz, J. K., Seshadri, A. and Khitatrakun, S. (2004), 'Are Americans saving "optimally" for retirement?', forthcoming in *Journal of Political Economy* (http://www.ssc.wisc.edu/~scholz/Research/Optimality.pdf).

Smith, J. P. (1999), 'Healthy bodies and thick wallets: the dual relation between health and economic status', *Journal of Economic Perspectives*, vol. 13, pp. 145–66.

University of Plymouth Library

Subject to status this item may be renewed
via your Voyager account

http://voyager.plymouth.ac.uk

Exeter tel: (01392) 475049
Exmouth tel: (01395) 255331
Plymouth tel: (01752) 232323

Prepared for Retirement?
The Adequacy and Distribution of
Retirement Resources in England

90 0986460 X

Published by
The Institute for Fiscal Studies
7 Ridgmount Street
London WC1E 7AE
tel. +44 (0) 20 7291 4800
fax +44 (0) 20 7323 4780
email: mailbox@ifs.org.uk
http://www.ifs.org.uk

Printed by
Patersons, Tunbridge Wells

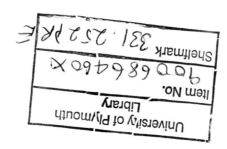